Goldmine's®
Essential Guide to
RECORD COLLECTING

DAVE THOMPSON

Published by

Krause Publications, a division of F+W Media, Inc.
700 East State Street • Iola, WI 54990-0001
715-445-2214 • 888-457-2873
www.krausebooks.com

To order books or other products call toll-free 1-800-258-0929
or visit us online at www.krausebooks.com

ISBN-13: 9781440248030
ISBN-10: 1440248036

Cover Design by Nicole MacMartin
Designed by Nicole MacMartin
Edited by Paul Kennedy

Printed in the United States of America.

10 9 8 7 6 5 4 3 2 1

CONTENTS

The Beatles are a nice start to any collection.
Courtesy Capitol Records

Thomas Edison listening to a wax cylinder phonograph at the Edison laboratory, Orange, New Jersey, 1888.

INTRODUCTION

THE BIRTH OF RECORD COLLECTING

PEOPLE HAVE BEEN COLLECTING RECORDS for as long as there have been records to collect.

In 1890, just a few years after Thomas Edison first marketed the wax cylinders that were the precursors of all that has been wrought since then, he also published the first catalog of available releases.

It was, admittedly a slender volume, but it included not only his company's releases, but also those produced by Columbia, the only other major player in town. And from these two innovations—one that might be all-but unrecognizable to the modern collector, another that would prove instantly familiar—the modern world of record collecting was born.

Cylinders were replaced by 78s, which in turn were supplanted by 45s and LPs. Rival formats (cassettes, eight tracks, CDs and mp3s) all came and went, and some of them had the temerity to come back again. Through it all, however, Edison's

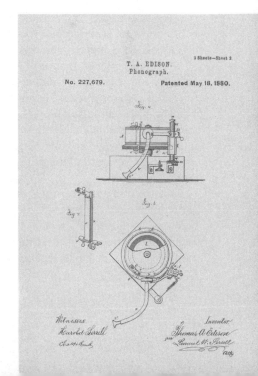

The patent drawing for Thomas Edison's phonograph, May 1880.

basic concept—of a piece of material, be it wax, shellac or vinyl, from which a stylus extracted the sounds of a performance—remains the most constant, and beloved, of them all.

The 78, the format that initially displaced the cylinder, was the invention of German-born Emile Berliner. Coming to the US in 1870 at 19, Berliner never saw Edison's fragile, bulky cylinders as anything but a first draft in the race to create the perfect musical medium, and he was correct. Easily broken, cylinders also wore out after just a few plays, until it was impossible to hear what was supposed to be on them.

Convinced that a more permanent medium must exist, and experimenting through the 1880s, Berliner unveiled the prototype of his "flat disc" in 1888 at the Franklin Institute. His earliest experiments involved etching the record's contents into zinc, using chromic acid. He then turned to celluloid and rubber, before finally settling upon shellac in 1891, and his work was complete. Shellac remained the industry standard for the next half-century.

And collectors have been collecting all along.

The fascination, of course, should be familiar to everyone. "Collecting" is as much a part of the so-called "human condition" as any other instinct, even if it has not always been recognized as such. What was Noah if not the first collector, gathering together two of every living creature, thousands of years before the Swedish scientist Carl Linnaeus set about formally naming them?

What were the Brothers Grimm if not collectors of every folk tale they could find in their native Germany?

The "antiquaries" of the 17th century collected relics of the past, be they books, coins, manuscripts, jewelry, ornaments, whatever, and from those enthusiasms, the attendant modern hobbies developed.

Harvard Professor Francis J Child collected ancient English and Scottish ballads, and published five volumes of them, filled with every different version of each song he could find.

The moment the first postage stamps appeared, people began to collect them—famously, the first stamp ever issued was Great Britain's Penny Black, in 1840, and it would be almost a year before a second one came along. And perhaps you're thinking that wouldn't make much of a collection; one stamp.

But the stamps were printed in sheets of 240, and each of those 240 had a different pair of letters printed in the bottom corners. One stamp becomes 240. Eleven different printing plates were employed, each with its own minute variations—240 stamps become 2640. One of those prints was damaged and needed to be repaired. More variations. One stamp becomes almost 3,000.

That is how collecting works, and that is how collectors think. Every different variety of a stamp. Every different issue of a magazine. Every different painting by an artist. In novelist Iain Sinclair's *White Chapell Scarlet Tracings*, we meet a bibliophile who is pursuing every edition of the Sherlock Holmes novel *The Sign of Four* that has ever been published. And in the documentary *Desperate Man Blues*, we meet Joe Bussard, who seems to be hunting down every "old time music" 78 ever made.

Whether stamps, Sherlock Holmes, or even 78s, there is joy in the pursuit. With record collecting the same rings true. There is joy in the hunt, the history, the treasure, and, must importantly, in the music. We will explore all of that, and more, in the following pages.

EDISON vs BERLINER
ANOTHER FORMAT WAR

THROUGHOUT THE LAST YEARS OF the 19th century, and into the first decades of the 20th, record collecting, and production, continued to grow. By 1924, when Thomas Edison's eponymous record label published the latest catalog of its own releases, the seven-by-five inch catalog totaled almost 500 pages and was an inch thick.

It also detailed, as so many catalogs do, then and now, the advantages inherent in its product… or, as it was described therein, "Thomas A Edison's Re-Creation of Music"…

Cylinders were dead, but Edison was not disheartened. Presaging the format wars that would later see VHS vanquish Betamax, cassettes kill off 8-Tracks and mp3s fend off so many rival digital formats, Edison never forgave flat 78s for upstaging his cylinders, and responded in exactly the manner you would expect him to. By

Edison ditched his beloved cylinder for a thick disc and thus began the music format wars.
Image courtesy Library of Congress

THE New Process Edison Records have a tone-
quality and a volume that places them beyond comparison. Ordinary records may perhaps suit him
who has the Phonograph temperament ; but Edison Records ONLY are for the critical one or for the enthusiast.

Record Lists everywhere.

The Edison Gem Phonograph (*improved*) is now on sale
at all dealers in talking machines. The New Model is
mounted on a polished hardwood base. The price, $10.00,
includes a dustproof carrying case, a separate reproducer and
a separate recorder.

Catalogues everywhere.

EIGHT DIFFERENT
MODELS FROM
$10.00
UP

NONE GENUINE
WITHOUT
THIS   TRADE MARK

THE NATIONAL
PHONOGRAPH
COMPANY
NEW YORK

launching a rival disc, as flat as a 78, but thicker and, or so he boasted, better
quality, too.

According to his catalog, "Edison Records are essentially different from
talking-machine records [as he termed 78s]. They are true representations
of vocal and instrumental music as produced by living artists. They are not
mere shadows. They are the very substance of the living music, alive with all
the emotions of the living artist. They are produced *through* a medium, not
by it."

All of which was true. But, by the end of the decade, they had been
discontinued. Only the collectors cared for them now.

They still do and, although there are not hordes of people searching for

them, those that are remain seriously dedicated. For the rest of us… well, you rarely see Edison discs and, even when you do, you're more likely to remark upon their size ("oh my goodness, that record must be a quarter of an inch thick!") than you are their contents ("Oh cool! Vernon Dalmart's 'The Wreck on the Southern Old 97.'")

They revolve at around 80 rpm. They are made of condensate, a compound made via the condensation process, and sprayed onto a celluloid base that was bonded to a wood flour core. And they could (or, at least, should) only be played with a diamond needle, affixed to a specialist Edison player. In terms of quality, durability and fidelity, Edison discs were so superior to other 78s that it wasn't funny. But they say that about Blu-Ray as well.

If you have the patience to pursue them, however, and the equipment on which to play them, collecting Edison Records is one of those pursuits that doesn't just get under your skin. It gets into your bloodstream, and the knowledge that you will probably never complete your collection just adds to the thrill.

This is record collecting at its most pure and primal, seeking out discs that are never less than nearly 90 years old, and some are well over a century; that can only be played on a certain type of player, and that steadfastly avoid almost every major musical bag that gets the rest of the collecting world so hot under the collar. This is devotion.

Launched in 1912, the first Edison discs—indeed, the first 10 years of Edison discs—rate among the most distinctive looking discs ever produced for the mass market: unless you look carefully, they are utterly indistinctive. Black discs with black molded labels.

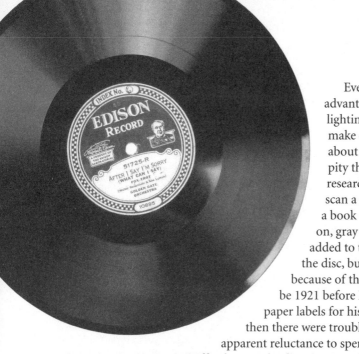

Even with all the advantages of modern lighting, it's difficult to make out what you're about to listen to, and pity the 21st century researcher wanting to scan a few to illustrate a book or a blog. Early on, gray highlighting was added to the lettering on the disc, but it was dropped because of the cost. It would be 1921 before Edison approved paper labels for his discs, and even then there were troubles – such as his apparent reluctance to spend money on glue to affix them to the discs.

Ah, but you jump through all the technological hoops and it is *so* worth the effort. According to the most complete modern catalogs, there were over 26,000 releases on the label between 1912 and its closure in 1929; and, while few of the myriad artists who recorded for Edison are household names today, in their day they were hot potatoes.

Early country connoisseurs *do* still seek out the aforementioned Vernon Dalmart. But vaudevillians John Orren and Lillian Drew; Hawaiian guitarists Helen Louise and Frank Ferrera; comedian Billy Golden and James Marlowe; soprano Rachael Grant; pianist Carlos Valderrama; the Jazzarimba Orchestra and the Green Brothers Novelty Band... what cares the modern music lover for them today?

Van Avery, "the Original Rastus." Gilbert Girard with his animal impressions. The Three Vagrants....

We believe, and correctly so, that the medium of recorded sound, like the printed word and the developed photograph, grants a certain immortality to its subjects and, to an extent, that is true.

But it also reminds us how easy it is for even the most feted celebrities to be utterly forgotten, particularly as there can be few, if any, people left alive today who purchased any but the last few years of the Edison label's output. Perhaps Arthur Fields' Assassinators lived up to their name a little too well.

There are some true jewels to be discovered, however. Novelty pianist Zez Confrey's eternally adorable "Kitten on the Keys." The Imperial Marimba Band's rendering of "12th Street Rag." Another Vernon Dalhart stormer, "Carolina Rolling Stone." The Premier Quartet's "Farmyard

Medley." A wealth of patriotic songs unfurled during the Great War (including yet another Dalhart gem, the truly marvelous "Lorraine (My Beautiful Alsace-Lorraine)." George Wilton Ballard's "Mother of Pearl."

We have no way of knowing how many Edison discs survive in collections and junk stores today; whether the titles that are to be noted online, selling on e-Bay or safely reposing in an archive some place, represent the mere tip of an iceberg of extant copies, or the last bold survivors of a long-exterminated pressing run.

In terms of musical impact, perhaps it doesn't matter whether there's just one copy of the New York Military Band's "American Eagle March" out there, or a thousand. So long as that one has been digitized for posterity, so nobody can accuse us of being cavalier with our heritage, it will always be there if someone should need to hear it.

Which is not the point, but it's better than nothing. Other fields of 78-and-related endeavor have seen the creation of censuses noting everything from the estimated number of copies that are "out there," to sad lists of the records that are known to have once existed, but which have yet to be rediscovered. Blues collectors are especially punctilious in that respect; Edison collectors not so much. And so we regret that Mr. Edison had little, if any, appreciation for "race records."

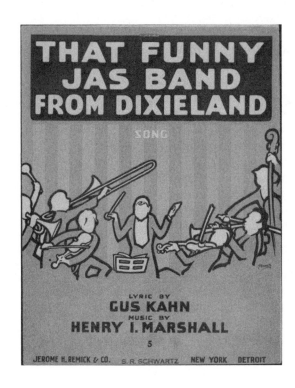

A number of what would have been termed "hot" titles did appear, and the catalog notes such early pioneers as the Frisco Jass Band, Red Nichols, Red & Miff's Stompers, Chas. Matson's Creole Serenaders, Clarence Williams and Eva Taylor, the Five Harmaniacs, Viola McCoy, Fletcher Henderson and Josie Miles. In fact, if you really want to get archaeological about it, the very first recorded mention of the word "jazz" (or thereabouts) came courtesy of an Edison disc, a 1916 effort by baritone Arthur F. Collins and tenor Byron G. Harlan, "That Funny Jas Band From Dixieland."

For the most part, however, Edison's A&R department targeted its output at the kind of audience that appreciated waltzes and foxtrots, accordion music and Polish polkas. The Russian pianist and composer Sergei Rachmaninov was an admirer of Edison, and recorded many sides for his label.

Other classical bodies followed him, for they agreed with Edison's own determination that the Edison disc offered a sonic step above anything available on other, cheaper or more popular record labels.

Which might be why the entire edifice came crumbling down in 1929. As other technologies advanced, Edison's remained the same. He pioneered what, by the day's standards, were long-playing discs, but refused to either share his technology with other manufacturers, or adapt his own so that Edison discs could be played on other gramophones. As other company's prices came down, Edison's went up.

Recording techniques improved, Edison's stayed the same. Add to that, the fact that the old man was more or less deaf as a post, and you can feel the frustration in his son Theodore's oft-quoted recollection of old Thomas listening to his competitors' records with the volume turned up full, and the speaker rattling with distortion. "He became so deaf that he couldn't hear that good electrical reproduction was possible."

It was 1929 before Edison finally agreed to make "compatible" records, around the same time as he decided to get out of the record label business. The last Edison discs were produced at the end of that same year, by which time the company's market share had shrunk to a mere fraction of what it had once been.

Not for the last time in the history of recorded sound, the public had been offered the choice between stunning fidelity and scratchy approximations, and taken the cheapest option.

While Edison faltered, other labels—utilizing that "other" format— flourished, including several that remain legendary today: Paramount, the home of some of the greatest blues records ever made; Gennett, Bluebird, Silvertone, Crown.

Were people actually, *actively*, collecting their releases, though? Yes, they were. Through the 1950s and 1960s, young blues fans like Canned Heat's Al Wilson and guitar legend John Fahey were among the enthusiasts who would make regular pilgrimages to the south, simply to bang on people's doors and ask whether they had any old records for sale.

They rarely came home empty-handed, either, and, more importantly than that, they often scored recordings that they had never dreamed existed,

78s that are still known to survive as just a handful of examples.

These hordes would not have existed without somebody in the household gathering them together in the first place, and whether that person would have described him or herself as a collector is irrelevant.

The very act of accumulation creates a collection, and so what if it was simply an assemblage of the songs that the owner liked the best? A painstakingly curated collection of "my favorite records" is as valid a specialty as a shelf full of first pressing Count Basie LPs.

Despite this, record collecting is generally regarded only to have become a formal pursuit in the early 1940s. That was when Big Joe Clauberg, a former circus strongman, opened what became the Jazz Record Center (but was originally called Joe's Juke Box) on New York's West 47th Street, not the first used record store in America, but certainly the most legendary.

With its shelves stocked with whatever records he could find, concentrating on jazz but allowing that definition to spread through blues, country and more, Big Joe's became a mecca for every enthusiast in the region and beyond, and a meeting place too. Marybeth Hamilton, whose *In Search of the Blues* remains one of the finest books ever written on its subject, captured the scene:

"Saturday afternoons they met at Indian Joe's, where they thumbed through the bins in between swigs from the bottles of muscatel that Pete Kaufman brought along from his [liquor] store...."

And Amanda Petrusich, whose *Do Not Sell At Any Price* is correspondingly among the greatest books ever written on the record collecting hobby, continues, "I can only imagine the half-furious half wheezy sounds eager collectors made clomping up [the steps], balls of cash wadded up in their pockets. Regardless of what the inside of the shop actually looked like, I like to imagine it crammed with weirdoes bickering in high pitched voices, nostrils expanding.... I like to imagine myself there, with a record or two tucked under my arm."

Don't we all?

So the Jazz Record Center was not the country, or even New York's first used record store. But it seems to have become the one to which the majority of collectors would gravitate, either on foot or, taking advantage of the adverts that Big Joe placed in such magazines as *Jazzways*, by mail.

Gathering his stock from wholesalers looking to dump surplus oldies, from passers-by looking to sell off their own abandoned collections of 78s, from any and every possible source, Big Joe attracted the cream of the nascent collecting world.

One of Big Joe's former employees, Henry Rinard, wrote a lovely piece about the store for *78 Quarterly*, in which he recalled the "specialists. One guy who just collected only European Jazz."

FIFTEEN AT SEVENTY-EIGHT
RARE BLUES FROM THE SHELLAC AGE

Long "Cleve" Reed & Harvey Hull (Down Home Boys): *Original Stack O' Lee Blues / Mama You Don't Know How* (Black Patti 8030, 1927) current value: **$60,000** *estimated*

Tommy Johnson: *Alcohol and Jake Blues / Ridin' Horse* (Paramount 12950, 1930) current value: **$30,000**

Long "Cleve" Reed & Little Harvey Hull (The Down Home Boys): *Gang of Brown Skin Women / Don't You Leave Me Here* (Black Patti 8002, 1927) current value: **$15,000**

Robert Johnson: *Me and the Devil Blues / Little Queen of Spades* (Vocalion 04108, 1938) current value: **$12,000**

There were others who sought only the sounds of New Orleans. Others still, who focused on single performers. They all descended, and they got to know one another, establishing friendships that developed into networks, all keeping an eye open for another's passions, then trading the scores that they came across.

The hobby was still in flux in those days. There were no price guides that told you what a specific record was worth; records were valued according to the seller's own awareness of how many copies he might have seen in the past, or the impressions he gleaned from other collectors or writers.

Nor was there any presentiment that 78s were not destined to last forever. But they weren't. By the end of the decade, a whole new recorded medium was moving in and, in precisely the same way as 78s had displaced cylinders, so LPs and singles were about to displace 78s.

Charley Patton: *Poor Me / 34 Blues* (Vocalion 02651, 1934) current value: **$10,000**

Mississippi John Hurt: *Frankie / Nobody's Dirty Business* (Okeh 8560, 1928) current value: **$7,500**

Robert Johnson: *Hell Hound on My Trail / From Four Until Late* (Vocalion 03623, 1937) current value: **$7,500**

Robert Johnson: *I Believe I'll Dust My Broom / Dead Shrimp Blues* (Vocalion 03475, 1937) current value: **$7,500**

Robert Johnson: *Come On in My Kitchen / They're Red Hot* (Vocalion 03563, 1937) current value: **$7,500**

Robert Johnson: *Malted Milk / Milkcow's Calf Blues* (Vocalion 03665, 1937) current value: **$6,000**

Robert Johnson: *Sweet Home Chicago / Walkin' Blues* (Vocalion 03601, 1937) current value: **$6,000**

Louie Lasky: *How You Want Your Rollin' Done / Teasin' Brown Blues* (Vocalion 02995, 1935) current value: **$5,000**

Tommy Johnson: *Canned Heat Blues / Big Fat Mamma Blues* (Victor V-38535, 1929) current value: **$4,000**

Cannon's Jug Stompers: *Pretty Mama Blues / Going to Germany* (Victor V-38535, 1930) current value: **$3,000**

Cannon's Jug Stompers: *Walk Right In / Whoa Mule! Get Up in the Alley* (Victor V-38___ 1930) current value: **$3,000**

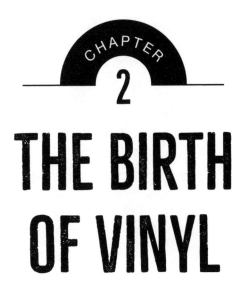

CHAPTER 2

THE BIRTH OF VINYL

THE NEW FORMATS WERE A REVOLUTION, and they caused one as well.

Playable on far smaller machines than any 78 player could ever have been, and made from a revolutionary fabric that was infinitely more durable than the fragile 78s, "vinyl" made its debut in 1948 when Columbia introduced the 10-inch long-playing record. The "album," as we know it today… and "the album" as record buyers of the time also knew it, although their concept was somewhat more literal than ours.

78s could carry just two songs, one track per side. Any release demanding more than that—a movie score, for example, or a lengthy classical work—would thus be forced either to condense their contents into a medley, or spread its wares across however many discs were required.

These would then be bundled up into single packages (we'd call them box sets today), but the nature of the packaging, with each disc in a separate sleeve, and all bound into an outer card cover, more closely resembled a scrapbook or a photo album. So that's how people termed them. They were "record albums."

The long-player, however, did exactly what it said. Instead of 12 songs being lavished across six discs, they were now spread across just one. And

Charlie Parker's 1949 *The Bird Blows The Blues,* is believed to be the first Jazz LP.
William Gottlieb/Getty Images

whereas those six discs might once have devoured a couple of inches of bookshelf, an "LP" required a mere fraction of the space.

The first 33-and-a-third long-playing (10-inch) records were actually produced as early as 1931 by RCA Victor and Columbia. They were, however, fraught with difficulties. RCA chose to employ a patent vinyl substance known as Victorlac, a vinyl compound that simply could not handle the weight of the average household pick-up—the business end of the turntable arm, wherein the stylus is housed. Just a couple of plays would see the needle gouge the record. After little more than a year of customer complaints, the records were withdrawn.

Columbia's efforts were no more successful, and both companies returned to the drawing board—one that was to be further complicated by the advent first of the Great Depression, and then the Second World war. It would be 15 years before the LP could finally be reintroduced.

Few of the earliest albums to be released, while not necessarily easy to find, are considered "rare" in terms of value. There is, however, at least one exception to the rule. Released in 1949, Charlie Parker's *Bird Blows the Blues* is widely believed to be the first Jazz LP ever released, and is valued accordingly. And other jazz artists swiftly migrated, likewise, to the new format: by the end of 1949, Count Basie, Billie Holliday, Gene Krupa and Duke Ellington all revolved at 33, taking advantage of the new format's sonic versatility to expand their musical horizons far beyond the confines of the old 78.

Classical music, too, would soon be leaping aboard a format that permitted works to be heard as a seamless whole, as opposed to being broken up across however many 78s were required. And, of course, by the mid-1960s, rock artists, too, were stretching in similar directions, the likes of the Rolling Stones' "Goin' Home" and Bob Dylan's "Sad Eyed Lady of the Lowlands" paving the way for side or even album-long songs and suites.

Other notable releases from the first pioneering months of the long-playing record include:

Bob Wills: *Round-Up* (Columbia CL9003, 1949) current value: **$300**

Roy Acuff: *Songs of the Smoky Mountains* (Columbia CL9004, 1949) current value: **$250**

Spade Cooley: *Sagebrush Swing* (Columbia CL9007, 1949) current value: **$250**

Frank Sinatra: *Christmas Songs by Sinatra* (Columbia CL6019, 1948) current value: **$200**

Gene Autry: *Western Classics, Volume 2* (Columbia HL9002, 1949) current value: **$175**

Bing Crosby: *Crosby Classics* (Columbia CL6027, 1949) current value: **$150**

Woody Herman: *Dance Parade* (Columbia CL6049, 1949) current value: **$140**

Eddy Howard: *Eddy Howard* (Columbia CL6067, 1949) current value: **$120**

Bob Atcher: *Early American Folk Songs* (Columbia HL9006, 1949) current value: **$100**

Claude Thornhill: *Dance Parade* (Columbia CL6050, 1949) current value: **$100**

Carson Robison: *Square Dance* (Columbia CL6029, 1949) current value: **$100**

Kay Kyser: *Campus Favorites* (Columbia CL6012, 1948) current value: **$100**

Benny Goodman and Peggy Lee: *Benny Goodman and Peggy Lee* (Columbia CL6033, 1949) current value: **$100**

Alvy West: *...and His Little Band* (Columbia CL6062, 1949) current value: **$75**

Dorothy Shay: *Sings* (Columbia CL6003, 1948) current value: **$50**

Xavier Cugat: *Cugat's Rhumba* (Columbia CL6005, 1948) current value: **$50**

Danny Kaye: *Danny Kaye* (Columbia CL6023, 1949) current value: **$50**

Dinah Shore: *...Sings* (Columbia CL6004, 1949) current value: **$50**

With the LP swiftly embedding itself into the marketplace, it was clear that the 78 at last had a viable challenger. However, the bulk of record sales in the United States were not for full-length albums, be they spread across six 78s or one 33. They were for single hit songs, and patently the LP was of no value there (more than two decades would elapse before the 12-inch single became reality).

An answer, however, was already at hand. In March 1949, the rival RCA label unveiled the "single," a seven-inch disc that spin at 45 rpm, and echoed the 78 format of one song, sometimes two, per side; while emphasizing the

Perry Como recorded the first 45 rpm song to top the charts with "'A' -- You're Adorable" in 1949.
Image courtesy Heritage Auctions

"unbreakability" of vinyl by also introducing turntables that allowed you to stack up to half a dozen records onto a center spindle, to each fall and play as the last one finished.

In theory, this too could amount to an album's worth of music and, in the very beginning, RCA seemed to think that that was the new format's primary goal—to rival the 33 with a more economically-sized "record album."

Swiftly, however, more logical thinking began to prevail.

There were almost 100 colored vinyl 45s included in that first wave of releases, all drawn from the ranks of the label's best selling 78s and spotlighting some of the biggest musical names, and most popular songs, of the day—Chet Atkins, Roy Rogers, Kitty Wells, Dale Evans, Spade Cooley and so many more. And while the label did not expect the 45 to displace the 78 immediately, the public leaped aboard the new innovation even more enthusiastically than they had the LP.

That May, barely two months after the format was unveiled, America had its first 45 rpm chart topper, Perry Como's "A: You're Adorable" (RCA 47-2899), and in November, the label was able to boast. "Coast to coast, teenagers are lining up for… neat little records they can slip in their pockets, with first class bands playing their favorite hits for 49c."

The album-sized ambition was abandoned. 45s were where the hits were made. Kids also, apparently, had bigger pockets back then.

Within months, other labels had leaped aboard the 45 bandwagon. Mercury, MGM and Capitol were among the first, with the latter rewarded for their enterprise when Frankie Laine's "The Cry of the Wild Goose" (5363-X45) gave them the format's first non-RCA number one. By 1952, more or less every record label in the land was producing 45s, and

The great Frankie Laine,
an early 45 star.
*Image courtesy John Springer
Collection/Getty Images*

in 1957, the new format's sales overtook those of 78s for the first time.

More than half a century of musical history went out of the window. Long before the end of the decade, 78s weren't simply on the way out, they were all but extinct in the US. They continued in production in the UK until around 1960, and elsewhere around the world into the mid-1960s—among the jewels in any Beatles collector's crown, for example, are the Fab Four 78s that were being released in India until as late as 1965.

But even there it was a dying art. Vinyl, whether revolving at 33 or 45 rpm, had taken over, and in the decades since then, it has withstood everything that technology can throw at it.

True, it marked its 50th anniversary, in the late 1990s, by being reduced to an underground sideshow behind the seemingly all-conquering compact disc. But out-of-sight never allowed it to fall out-of-mind.

The tables and booths at record fairs—the modern, worldwide, equivalent of the old Jazz Record Center—still creaked beneath the accumulated weight of five-decades worth of old LPs and singles; and the people who attended them, the latter-day incarnation of Petrusich's old-time "weirdoes" were still "bickering in high pitched voices," still surveying their domain with "nostrils expanding."

Still sniffing out their specialties.

THE FIRST 45s

Eddy Arnold: *Bouquet of Roses/Texarkana Baby* (RCA Victor 48-0001, 1949) current value: **$100 (with picture sleeve)**

Eddy Arnold: *Anytime/What a Fool I Was* (RCA Victor 48-0002, 1949) current value: **$60**

Pee Wee King: *Tennessee Waltz/Rootie Tootie*(RCA Victor 48-0003, 1949) current value: **$40**

Sons of the Pioneers: *Cool Water/Chant of the Wanderer* (RCA Victor 48-0004, 1949) current value: **$40**

Sons of the Pioneers: *Tumbling Tumbleweeds/Everlasting Hills of Oklahoma* (RCA Victor 48-0005, 1949) current value: **$40**

Sons of the Pioneers: *Trees/The Timber Trail* (RCA Victor 48-0006, 1949) current value: **$40**

Sons of the Pioneers: *Blue Prairie/Cowboy Camp Meetin'* (RCA Victor 48-0007, 1949) current value: **$40**

Roy Rogers: *Don't Fence Me In/Roll On Texas Moon* (RCA Victor 48-0008, 1949) current value: **$50**

Roy Rogers: *The Yellow Rose of Texas/On the Old Spanish Trail* (RCA Victor 48-0009, 1949) current value: **$50**

Roy Rogers: *San Fernando Valley/Along the Navajo Trail* (RCA Victor 48-0010, 1949) current value: **$50**

Roy Rogers: *Home in Oklahoma/A Gay Ranchero* (RCA Victor 48-0011, 1949) current value: **$50**

Cecil Campbell: *Steel Guitar Ramble/Left All Alone with a Broken Heart* (RCA Victor 48-0014, 1949) current value: **$50**

Eddy Arnold: *I'm Thinking Tonight of My Blue Eyes/Rockin' Alone* (RCA Victor 48-0016, 1949) current value: **$60**

Eddy Arnold: *It Makes No Difference Now/Molly Darling* (RCA Victor 48-0017, 1949) current value: **$60**

Eddy Arnold: *The Prisoner's Song/Seven Years with the Wrong Woman* (RCA Victor 48-0018, 1949) current value: **$60**

Eddy Arnold: *Will the Circle Be Unbroken/Who at My Door Is Standing* (RCA Victor 48-0019, 1949) current value: **$60**

Six Fat Dutchmen: *Dutchman's Waltz/Schneider Polka* (RCA Victor 48-0020, 1949) current value: **$60**

Henri Rene and his Musette Orchestra: *Jalousie/Hora Staccato* (RCA Victor 48-0021, 1949) current value: **$30**

Johnny Vadnal and his Orchestra: *She Told Me—Polka/Dancer's Waltz* (RCA Victor 48-0022, 1949) current value: **$30**

Six Fat Dutchmen: *Old Lady Polka/Saturday Waltz* (RCA Victor 48-0023, 1949) current value: **$30**

Henri Rene and his Musette Orchestra/Lawrence Duchow and his Red Raven Orchestra: *Helen/Yes Yes Polka* (RCA Victor 48-0024, 1949) current value: **$30**

Eddy Arnold: *A Heart Full of Love* (For a Handful of Kisses)/Then I Turned and Walked Slowly Away (RCA Victor 48-0025, 1949) current value: **$60**

Eddy Arnold: *Just a Little Lovin'* (Will Go a Long, Long Way)/My Daddy Is Only a Picture (RCA Victor 48-0026, 1949) current value: **$60**

Spade Cooley: *The Best Deal in Town/Spanish Fandango* (RCA Victor 48-0027, 1949) current value: **$50**

Roy Rogers: *My Heart Went That-a-Way/No Children Allowed* (RCA Victor 48-0028, 1949) current value: **$60**

Henri Rene and his Orchestra: *Mexican Hat Dance/Adios, Pampa Mia!* (RCA Victor 48-0029, 1949) current value: **$30**

Eddy Arnold: *I'll Hold You in My Heart* (Till I Can Hold You in My Arms)/Don't Bother to Cry (RCA Victor 48-0030, 1949) current value: **$60**

Jim Boyd: *We Were Married/Mule Boogie* (RCA Victor 48-0031, 1949) current value: **$50**

Spade Cooley: *Call Me Darlin' Do/Four Fiddle Polka* (RCA Victor 48-0032, 1949) current value: **$50**

The Georgia Crackers: *A Broken Doll/That's the Way It's Gonna be* (RCA Victor 48-0033, 1949) current value: **$80**

Roy Rogers: *The Kid with the Rip in His Pants/Dusty* (RCA Victor 48-0034, 1949) current value: **$60**

Roy Rogers: *Blue Shadows on the Trail/*(There'll Never Be Another) Pecos Bill (RCA Victor 48-0035, 1949) current value: **$60**

Blue Sky Boys: *Dust on the Bible/Speak to Me Little Darling* (RCA Victor 48-0036, 1949) current value: **$60**

Pee Wee King: *Bull Fiddle Boogie/Chattanooga Bus* (RCA Victor 48-0037, 1949) current value: **$40**

The Harmoneers Quartet: *Rock Of Ages/Tell Me The Old, Old Story* (RCA Victor 48-0038, 1949) current value: **$25**

The Harmoneers Quartet: *The Church In The Wildwood/Have Thine Own Way Lord* (RCA Victor 48-0039, 1949) current value: **$25**

The Harmoneers Quartet: *I Love To Tell The Story/Just As I Am* (RCA Victor 48-0040, 1949) current value: **$25**

Joe Biviano: *Manhattan Hop/N.B.C. Polka* (RCA Victor 48-0041, 1949) current value: **$40**

Eddy Arnold: *There's Not a Thing* (I Wouldn't Do for You)/Don't Rob Another Man's Castle (RCA Victor 48-0042, 1949) current value: **$60**

Spade Cooley: *Texas Playboy Rag/Lord Nottingham's War Dance* (RCA Victor 48-0043, 1949) current value: **$50**

Elton Britt: *Maybe I'll Cry Over You/In a Swiss Chalet* (RCA Victor 48-0044, 1949) current value: **$50**

Merrie Musette: *Bar Room Polka/The Miller's Daughter* (RCA Victor 48-0045, 1949) current value: **$20**

Charlie Monroe: *Rosa Lee McFall/They Didn't Believe It Was True* (RCA Victor 48-0046, 1949) current value: **$50**

Jim Boyd: *Dear John/One Heart, One Love* (RCA Victor 48-0047, 1949) current value: **$50**

Elton Britt: *Lorelei/Rainbow in My Heart* (RCA Victor 48-0049, 1949) current value: **$50**

The Carter Sisters: *Someone's Last Way/Why Do You Weep Dear Willow* (RCA Victor 48-0050, 1949) current value: **$50**

The Georgia Crackers: *Gone Down the Drain/In One Ear and Out the Other* (RCA Victor 48-0051, 1949) current value: **$80**

Zeke Manners: *There Is Nothin' Like a Dame/When It's Springtime in the Rockies* (RCA Victor 48-0052, 1949) current value: **$50**

The Fat Dutchmen: *Fat Man's Polka/Skal Skal Skal—Waltz* (RCA Victor 48-0053, 1949) current value: **$20**

Slim Montana: *Bluebird on Your Windowsill/All I Need Is Some More Lovin'* (RCA Victor 48-0054, 1949) current value: **$50**

Johnnie and Jack: *She Went with a Smile/Trials and Tribulations* (RCA Victor 48-0055, 1949) current value: **$50**

Hank Snow: *Marriage Vow/The Star Spangled Waltz* (RCA Victor 48-0056, 1949) current value: **$50**

Shorty Long: *The Morning After/Please Daddy Forgive* (RCA Victor 48-0057, 1949) current value: **$50**

Ernie Lee: *Keep Walking/Pray, Pray, Pray* (RCA Victor 48-0058, 1949) current value: **$40**

Ernie Benedict & his Polkateers: *Polka Dots and Polka Dreams/Tzigane Polka* (RCA Victor 48-0059, 1949) current value: **$30**

Sons of the Pioneers: *Room Full of Roses/Riders in the Sky* (RCA Victor 48-0060, 1949) current value: **$40**

Dave Denney: *Lord Protect My Darling/You Big Bouquet of Roses* (RCA Victor 48-0061, 1949) current value: **$40**

Chet Atkins: *Guitar Waltz/Barber Shop Rag* (RCA Victor 48-0062, 1949) current value: **$60**

Spade Cooley: *The Gal I Left Behind Me/Arkansas Traveler* (RCA Victor 48-0063, 1949) current value: **$50**

Elton Britt & Rosalie Allen: *Tennessee Yodel Polka/Swiss Lullaby* (RCA Victor 48-0064, 1949) current value: **$50**

Rosalie Allen and Elton Britt with The Skytoppers: *Tennessee Yodel Polka/Swiss Lullaby* (RCA Victor 48-0065, 1949) current value: **$20**

Bill Boyd and His Cowboy Ramblers: *Blue Danube Waltz/Varsoviana* (RCA Victor 48-0067, 1949) current value: **$50**

Rosalie Allen: *The Yodeling Bird/Square Dance Polka* (RCA Victor 48-0068, 1949) current value: **$50**

Slim Whitman: *Please Paint a Rose on the Garden Wall/Tears Can Never Drown the Flame* (RCA Victor 48-0069, 1949) current value: **$70**

Lawrence Duchow and his Red Raven Orchestra: *Milwaukee Polka/Land O' Lakes Sweetheart* (RCA Victor 48-0070, 1949) current value: **$20**

Texas Jim Robertson: *Slipping Around/Wedding Bells* (RCA Victor 48-0071, 1949) current value: **$50**

Blue Sky Boys: *Alabama/You've Branded Your Name on My Heart* (RCA Victor 48-0072, 1949) current value: **$60**

Dale Evans: *Don't Ever Fall in Love with a Cowboy/Nothin' in My Letter Box* (RCA Victor 48-0073, 1949) current value: **$60**

Roy Rogers: *Home on the Range/That Palomino Pal of Mine* (RCA Victor 48-0074, 1949) current value: **$60**

Homer and Jethro: *Baby, It's Cold Outside/Country Girl* (RCA Victor 48-0075, 1949) current value: **$60**

Cecil Campbell: *Tropical Island/Tar Heel Rag* (RCA Victor 48-0076, 1949) current value: **$50**

Spade Cooley: *The Wagoner/Wake Up Susan* (RCA Victor 48-0077, 1949) current value: **$50**

Spade Cooley: *Flop Eared Mule/The Eighth of January* (RCA Victor 48-0078, 1949) current value: **$50**

Spade Cooley: *Ida Red/Six Eight to the Barn* (RCA Victor 48-0079, 1949) current value: **$50.**

Eddy Arnold: *I'm Throwing Rice* (At the Girl That I Love)/Show Me the Way Back to Your Heart (RCA Victor 48-0080, 1949) current value: **$60**

Dude Martin: *I Always Had A Way With Women/Nevada Waltz* (RCA Victor 48-0081, 1949) current value: **$40**

Eddy Arnold: *One Kiss Too Many/The Echo of Your Footsteps* (RCA Victor 48-0083, 1949) current value: **$60**

Kitty Wells: *Love or Hate/Don't Wait for the Last Minute to Pray* (RCA Victor 48-0084, 1949) current value: **$70**

Pee Wee King: *Tennessee Polka/The Nashville Waltz* (RCA Victor 48-0085, 1949) current value: **$40**

Homer and Jethro: *Waltz with Me/Roll Along Kentucky Moon* (RCA Victor 48-0086, 1949) current value: **$50**

The Harmoneers Quartet: *I Want To Go There/I've Been List'ning In On Heaven* (RCA Victor 48-0087, 1949) current value: **$30**

Hank Snow: *The Blind Boy's Dog/Anniversary of My Broken Heart* (RCA Victor 48-0088, 1949) current value: **$50**

Chet Atkins: *Dance of the Goldenrod/Telling My Troubles to My Old Guitar* (RCA Victor 48-0089, 1949) current value: **$60**

Slim Montana: *Streamlined Yodel Song/My Swiss Moonlight Lullaby* (RCA Victor 48-0090, 1949) current value: **$50.00**

Elton Britt: *Reaching for the Moon/Two Hearts Are Better Than One* (RCA Victor 48-0091, 1949) current value: **$50**

Ernie Lee: *You Can't Pick A Rose In December/One, Two, Three* (RCA Victor 48-0092, 1949) current value: **$30**

Jim Boyd: *Dust on My Telephone/Save the Next Waltz for Me* (RCA Victor 48-0093, 1949) current value: **$50**

Sons of the Pioneers: *Rounded Up in Glory/Too High, Too Wide, Too Low* (RCA Victor 48-0094, 1949) current value: **$40**

Sons of the Pioneers: *Lead Me Gently Home Father/Power in the Blood* (RCA Victor 48-0095, 1949) current value: **$40**

Sons of the Pioneers: *The Old Rugged Cross/Read the Bible Every Day* (RCA Victor 48-0096, 1949) current value: **$40**

Texas Jim Robertson: *I Heard the Angels Weep/I'm So Low* (RCA Victor 48-0097, 1949) current value: **$40**

Shorty Long: *The Warm Red Wine/I Got Mine* (RCA Victor 48-0098, 1949) current value: **$50**

Jesse Rogers: *Blue Christmas/Here Comes Santa Claus* (RCA Victor 48-0100, 1949) current value: **$60**

Sons of the Pioneers: *Lie Low Little Doggies/Bar None Ranch* (RCA Victor 48-0101, 1949) current value: **$40**

Dude Martin: *My Tennessee Baby/Old Doc Brown* (RCA Victor 48-0102, 1949) current value: **$50**

Charlie Monroe: *Our Mansion Is Ready/A Valley of Peace* (RCA Victor 48-0103, 1949) current value: **$50**

Hank Snow: *My Filipino Rose/The Law of Love* (RCA Victor 48-0104, 1949) current value: **$50**

3

GRADING

VINYL

CONDITION, WE ARE OFTEN TOLD, is everything. And it is true. Condition is what separates a pristine disc from a scratched-to-death one; condition is how we determine whether a record is worth $1,000 or $1.

But determining condition—"grading," as it is known—is not an exact science. No matter how thoroughly you inspect a record, and no matter how carefully you listen to one, the flaws that you detect might be invisible to someone else; and the flaws you overlook might be poison to another. With the best will in the world, and the most analytical approach to the subject, the stated condition of any record being sold is at best a guide, and at worst, subjective.

Yet it is also the most important detail in any description of a record, or indeed, anything else that is being purchased online, unseen, from a stranger—and, alongside shipping costs and packaging, the one most likely to lead to disappointment or worse. Which is why when purchasing records online *always* check a seller's feedback, and *always* check the terms of sale. You won't rule out every potential problem, but at least you'll know if anyone else has run into difficulties.

Established two decades ago, the *Goldmine* Grading Guide is considered

As with beauty, record grading by novices is often in the eye of the beholder.

the standard in the marketplace. There are eight basic points on the *Goldmine* grading scale: Mint (M), Near Mint (NM), Very Good Plus (VG+), Very Good (VG), Good Plus (G+), Good (G), Fair (F) and Poor (P). Some dealers may insert their own intermediary grades—Near Mint Minus (NM-), for example, or Very Good Double Plus (VG++)—echoing the similar system that has operated in numismatics for many years; but these definitions vary from seller to seller.

A record grading Mint should be absolutely perfect in every regard. The record has certainly never been played, and could (some collectors say *should*) still be sealed in its original shrink-wrap. To these enthusiasts, the very act of opening (or, even worse, removing) the shrink-wrap immediately reduces a record to Near Mint, although even that is no guarantee of a pristine piece of vinyl.

Several years ago, a record store-owning correspondent to *Goldmine*'s "Spin Cycle" vinyl column wrote, "We cringe every time someone opens certain records in the store. I have seen VG pressings come out of a brand new Adele *21* LP. Mumford and Sons was not any better. These pressings are blatantly mishandled during manufacturing.

"We have seen multiple fingernail scratches, scuffs that run along all tracks; you name it I have seen it. Being a big collector of '60s to '90s records, I buy a lot of sealed original records from conventions where I set up. I have *never* opened a sealed [vintage] record that looked as bad as these new pressings do."

New releases, however, are not the only albums that refuse to adhere to the definitions of "new." Every buyer, no matter their age, can recall at least one occasion when they rushed home with a brand new purchase, only to find it warped or skipping, or missing the lyric sheet, or possessed of any of many other failings. And if they're in that state on the day they were unloaded from the distributor's truck, imagine all that could have happened to an album sitting still-sealed in a warehouse or forgotten

Even a high-demand album such as The Beatles' *Yesterday and Today* can be deemed almost worthless because of poor condition.

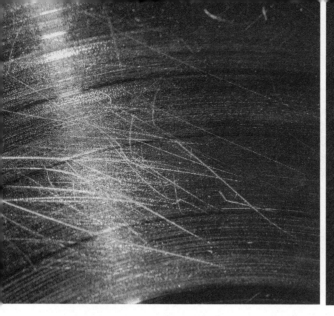

in a box for upwards of thirty years!

"Mint" is the ultimate *caveat emptor*… Buyer Beware!

Near Mint, then, is the grade that many dealers prefer to use, suggesting a record that is *almost* perfect. It is also the highest grade listed in all of the *Goldmine* price guides, with the understanding that any record that does exceed this standard will be worth significantly more than its stated value.

What can you expect from a Near Mint record? Near-perfection. It may possess the odd minor defect—a tiny (read all-but-invisible) trace of ring wear to the cover, the odd stray fingerprint or, around the spindle hole in the center of the record, a few silvery lines.

What there should *not* be are creases, folds, tears, splits, scratches, scribbles, dings or clicks. There will be no cutout hole (denoting that a record was once sold at a discount); there will be no overt indication whatsoever that this is anything but a new record that somebody opened before you received it.

The next grade is Very Good Plus (VG+). Generally valued at around 50% of the Near Mint value, the record will clearly have been played and otherwise handled by a previous owner, but it will also have been very well looked after. There may be some visible flaws—scuffs or surface scratches that cannot be felt with a fingertip, but these will not be audible.

A slight warp may be present, but again, it will not affect the music. There will be some wear to the label,

and more of those silvery lines, but the spindle hole itself will not appear misshapen from repeated plays. The sleeve may show some wear, but nothing to get excited about, while this is also the highest level at which a cut-out should be graded, no matter how pristine the rest of the package might be. Think of it as Near Mint with a few problems.

Famously, there are several records, particularly in the world of 78s, for which VG+ is the only condition that has ever been seen—Tommy Johnson's "Alcohol and Jake Blues" (Paramount 12950), for example.

But there are far more recent examples than that where, although exceptions may exist, they do so in very small quantities. The Raspberries' self-titled 1972 debut album with its scratch and sniff sticker (something approximating raspberries, naturally) unscratched, is one example; another

would be a copy of Public Image Ltd's *Metal Box* album, released in 1979 in a worldwide limited edition of 60,000 (of which 50,000 were intended for the domestic UK market).

Unlike the familiar two disc US pressing, *Second Edition*, this version featured three 12-inch, 45rpm, singles encased, indeed, in a pristine silver-colored circular metal box.

At least, it was pristine when it was issued. Almost 40 years later, finding a copy that has not at least begun the disfiguring oxidization process is akin to hunting down any of the hobby's other greatest rarities, while most now look like they've finished the process, and the only thing holding the tin together is the rust.

True, many collectors now believe the box was *intended* to rust, basing their suspicions on the later CD release of *The Complete Bill Evans on Verve*. That, too, was released in a metal box, with its inevitable oxidation publicized as one of its selling points! But *Metal Box* remains a collectible item, though. Even with more than half its surface covered in crumbly brown yuck, it remains valued in the region of $200. (*Metal Box* was reissued in 2016, this time in a square box. It is too soon, at the time of writing, to know whether this box, too, will rust itself into a state of disgrace.)

In both of these instances, you will notice, it is the packaging, as opposed to the record(s) that decree the album's overall condition and, for that reason, many responsible sellers choose to grade record and sleeve separately. Nevertheless, a NM record in a VG+ sleeve is exactly what it says. Seriously flawed.

Very Good (VG) tends to amplify the problems found in VG+, and tends to be worth around 25% of the Near Mint value. Expect to hear surface noise in places, particularly during the quieter moments, or during the intro or outro to songs, and scratches elsewhere will be audible. But the record will not skip, and none of these extraneous sounds will overpower the sound of the music itself.

Sure signs of a previous owner will be visible—writing, tape or stickers on either the label or the cover, although not necessarily to the detriment of either—a name written carefully in the top corner of the back cover, for example. (But not an artist's autograph. Personally signed LP sleeves can withstand almost any amount of abuse for as long as the autograph itself remains intact and genuine. For in these instances, it is oftentimes not the record being sold. It is the signature.)

There will be wear to the label, and to the cover itself—the edges will no longer be clean, the spine may show some wear. It's still a good looking, nice sounding record, but it once looked and sounded much better.

A record graded as Good, or Good Plus, will continue to amplify the aforementioned problems. Scratches and surface noise will be louder, although the record still should not skip. The grooves will look worn, and there will be some deterioration in the sound. The cover will be tatty, with split seams; the spine may be crushed and all but unreadable; and any amount of writing might now adorn the sleeve although that, in itself, is not such a terrible thing.

Several collectors have mentioned how much they enjoy owning records that, as one put it, "look more like the cover of a High School exercise book than anything else"—adolescent declarations of love for the artist, for example. Birthday greetings from one friend to another. Favorite songs highlighted and underlined; least favorites crossed out with bold slashes of ink. Faces are defaced and doodles drift across the artwork. There is a wonderful *human* aspect to records like this, a tiny slice of social history.

Do not despise them. Save that for records graded Poor (P) or Fair (F). The record will be scratched to pieces, possibly cracked, maybe warped, and will not play through without skipping or sticking.

The tattered, battered sleeve will scarcely hold the record any longer, and might well show signs of some other near-calamity—water damage, for example, or cigarette burns. Nothing about this record recommends itself to a purchaser… unless, of course, you want it. In which case, five percent of its NM value is the maximum you should pay.

Unless, of course, you *really* want it.

Because grading offers us guidelines, but that's all it can do. It does not make laws as well.

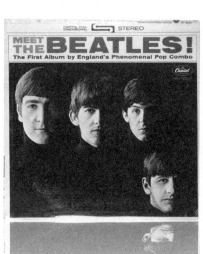

YESTERDAY AND TODAY

NEW VINYL SALES ARE STRONGER than they have been at any time since the mid-late 1980s, when the compact disc first started to encroach on its territory. But even if they weren't, vinyl itself would be as healthy as it has ever been, for "new" vinyl tells only a part of the story.

Yes, more new releases (and new reissues) are appearing every year, often in the most eye-catching packaging, and frequently retailing at eye-watering prices—box sets comprising great swathes of an individual artist's career seem to appear on an almost weekly basis, all of them offering a one-stop solution to every collector's wants list.

Albums that were so fabulously rare that some fans had never seen them (a mono pressing of the Rolling Stones' *Let It Bleed*, for example); others that never even got past the planning stage (the Beach Boys' *Smile*, David Bowie's *The Gouster*).

So many hitherto unimaginable albums are available and accessible today that it seems impossible to believe there was ever a time when such things were merely fables related around post-record show campfires, about the "friend of a friend of a friend" who once found…

…I don't know, a Velvet Underground acetate in a New York City dumpster, and discovered that it was an unreleased version of that band's very first album. Because now you can go online, or down to the record store, and pick up a copy of that self-same acetate, and hear for yourself

what collectors once dreamed of.

But how much more exciting would it be to have found that acetate in the first place? Or any other album that you've been hunting for years, even decades, tucked unassumingly away in a thrift store dollar bin, or carelessly filed in a record store basement, in a box with multiple copies of *Frampton Comes Alive*, the soundtrack to *Saturday Night Fever*, and any number of Seals and Croft long players?

Because, to many people, that's what vinyl collecting is *really* all about—not the collecting, *per se,* but the finding. The thrill of the hunt. And whether you're deep in the depths of darkest suburbia, pursuing Gaston County hillbillies by the light of a flickering forty watt bulb; or pushing through the crowds of similarly dedicated crate-divers, wondering whether today is the day you'll finally come across a first, uncensored pressing of the debut *Jefferson Airplane* album, it's the hunt that keeps you going.

Others, however, have their own definition of what the hobby means. For some, it's an investment. For others, it's a lifestyle. And for some, it's an obsession—one without which their lives would be as empty as their bank accounts, presumably, would be full.

Some people specialize, devoting their time to the pursuit of picture discs, or colored vinyl, or import 12-inch singles. Some indulge themselves in Chicago blues, in punk rock, in country. Some seek only first pressings on the jazz-centric Blue Note label; others will gather anything released by Sub

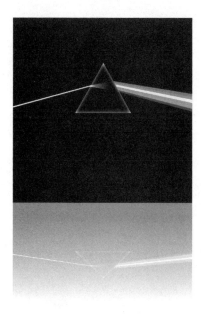

Pop or the black label years of Nipper the dog.

There are Sinatra collectors who can reel off the matrix numbers that are scratched in the "dead wax" (the blank plastic between grooves and label) of every album as though they were telephone numbers that they call everyday.

There are Grateful Dead collectors who have gathered up a vinyl recounting of every show they ever attended. There are Carter Family fans that only want records that have been autographed by a band member.

Record collecting is a science, an ever-unfolding microcosm of music and marketing—there are people who will only collect records that still have the manufacturer's "hype sticker" on the sleeve.

It is a sociological study—there are those who file their records not alphabetically by artist, but by release date, tracing shelf-by-shelf from the first days of rock 'n' roll through the British Invasion and psychedelia, from the singer-songwriter boom through the heyday of disco and onto the new world of the new wave.

It is a journal of your own life, tracing from the first record that you ever bought, all the way to your most recent purchases; and a record of your quirkiness, too—exactly how many versions of Gustav Holt's *The Planets* does one person really need? Or Pink Floyd's *Dark Side of the Moon,* for that matter? (Well, there's the original with all the posters and stickers; there's the quadraphonic pressing; there's a couple of reissues with sleeve varia-

Yessongs, a live album by Yes from 1973, features the artwork of English artist Roger Dean.
Image courtesy Heritage Auctions

tions; there's the remastered vinyl; and a few CDs, there's the box set with the bonus marbles, and the SACD… ummm…..)

It's anything and everything that you want it to be. You don't even have to like music to collect records. There are people who collect the artwork alone—fifties designs by Andy Warhol, seventies fantasies by Roger Dean; intricate sketching by George Underwood; gorgeous photographs by Annie Liebovitz; 21st century masterpieces by Gregory Curvey.

We collect individual artists… Woody Guthrie and Cyndi Lauper, Robert Johnson and the Mississippi Sheiks, Shostakovich and Sibelius. We pursue individual producers… Phil Spector, Joe Meek, Todd Rundgren, Bob

Brian Jones Presents the Pipes of Pan at Joujouka, a 1971 release of Moroccan music on Rolling Stones Records.

Ezrin…. Conductors and orchestras. Genres and labels, forgotten fashions and Rolling Stones spin-offs. All those Bill Wyman solo albums, Mick and Keith, too. Ronnie Wood, Mick Taylor… *Brian Jones Presents the Pipes of Pan at Joujouka.*

Short-lived formats and conversation-starting gimmicks fascinate. We've already mentioned twelve-inch singles, but there's a world of other sizes, too—five-inch and six-inch discs made great novelty releases in the late 1970s; and shaped discs, too. Who needs a boxful of boring old round ones when you could have every other geometric configuration under the sun?

There's other fabrics, too, beyond the familiar vinyl—lightweight flexi discs, Polish postcards, records pressed on X-Ray film, or on the back of breakfast cereal boxes. Back in 1972, the Himalayan nation of Bhutan even issued a series of playable postage stamps! They were too small, unfortunately, for most record players to handle, but if you were to play one, you might hear an encyclopedia-like account of Bhutan's geography and politics, or a thirty-second snatch of local music. How many future World Music collectors got their start via a pen friend from the Bhutanese capital of Thimphu? Or via a childhood fascination with philately?

But enough with the examples and suppositions. Suffice to say, there are almost as many different forms of record collecting, and reasons for it, too, as there are record collectors to begin with, and many (but not all—how dreadful it would be, after all, if everyone agreed on something?) will acknowledge that there has never been a more exciting time to pursue the hobby than today.

True, the rarities are more expensive now, and the obscurities are more obscure. "If I'd known then what I know now…" is one of the seasoned collector's most familiar laments, as he or she surveys the sums for which such-and-such a record now sells for, while recalling the day, many years ago, that they completely ignored the box full of copies being sold for a buck at their local record store.

But the Internet has opened the market wider than could ever have been imagined even twenty years ago; and though there may not be as many bricks-and-mortar record stores standing as there were back in the seventies and eighties, or as many record fairs taking place as there used to be in the nineties, there are more opportunities to buy, and sources to buy from, then ever before. Especially if you're willing to build the cost of shipping into your budget, as well.

It may (and, indeed, does) hurt to know that you are often paying more to the mailman than you are to the seller, especially when the record(s) you're buying are priced at the lower end of the spectrum.

But maybe the pleasure of crossing them off the wants list more than compensates for that. After all, if the disc in question was that easy to find *without* that added cost, you'd already have a copy. Wouldn't you?

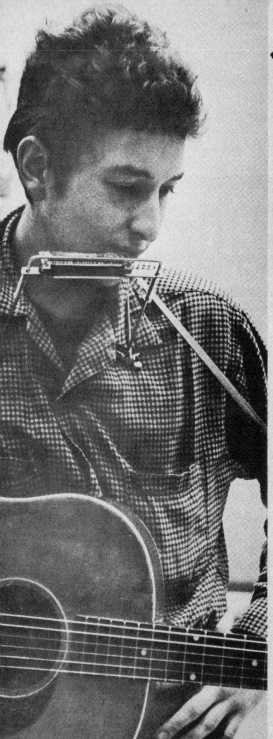

HAROLD LEVENTHAL presents

Bob Dylan

AT TOWN HALL

123 W. 43rd St.

FRI. EVE., APRIL 12th 1963 at 8:30 P.M

Tickets 3.00, 2.75, 2.00 on sale at Town Hall Box Office &
Folklore Center, 110 MacDougal St., GR 7-5987

"BOB DYLAN is . . . the most exciting, mo
potentially great new city Folksinger in rece
years. He is absolutely unique . . ."
—LITTLE SANDY REVI

"Among the trends is BOB DYLAN . . . this 2
year-old ragamuffin minstrel's songs contin
to captivate this listener . . . his songs a
musically well proportioned . . ."
—NEW YORK TIM

"He's so goddam real, it's unbelievable"
—SING O

"One of the most compelling blues singe
ever recorded"
—BBC RADIO TIM

". . . the very best of the newest generatio
of citybillies"
—HI/FI STEREO REVI

Columbia Records

The 1963 Bob Dylan concert in New York is considered the
first major live performance of his career, coming only a month
before *The Freewheelin' Bob Dylan* is released.
Image courtesy Heritage Auctions

5

MONEY
(THAT'S WHAT I SPEND)

THE ACTUAL *COST* OF COLLECTING is not a topic that this book is going to delve into too far.

You alone know what a record is worth to you; whether you are willing to pay what a dealer is asking, or would prefer to hold on for a cheaper (or better) copy; you alone know how much of your disposable income is, in fact, *that* disposable.

Most collectors are, after all, what one might call "amateur," with no more commercial connection to the hobby than is actually required by the act of buying what someone else is selling.

Yes, many of us like to think that, should the need ever arise, a well cared for collection can be sold for at least what we paid for it, and maybe it can. At the same time, however, we are also aware that the amount we paid for something is often the amount that it is worth, and when was the last time a dealer handed over a check with no hope whatsoever of making a profit on the transaction?

Certainly there are some (even many) records that will never lose their value; that can be resold at any time with some expectation of profit.

Back in 1994, in the third edition of *Goldmine's Price Guide to Collectible Record Albums*, the "100 Most Valuable US Albums" included the following:

Bob Dylan: *The Freewheelin' Bob Dylan;* (Columbia label original pressing featuring "Talking John Birch Blues," "Let Me Die in my Footsteps," "Rocks and Gravel" and "Gamblin' Willie's Dead Man's Hand": **$20,000 (stereo), $10,000 (mono)**

The Beatles: *The Beatles and Frank Ifield Onstage* (Veejay label. Beatles painting on cover) (stereo): **$9,000**

The Beatles: *Introducing The Beatles* (Vee-Jay label original featuring "Love Me Do" and "PS I Love You; ads for other Vee-Jay releases on reverse) (stereo): **$8,000**

The Beatles: *Yesterday and Today* (Capitol label. "Butcher" cover): **$7,500**

Ike & Tina Turner: *River Deep Mountain High* (Philles label): **$7,500**

Frank Ballard: *Rhythm-Blues Party* (Phillips Int'l label): **$4,500**

Boyd Bennett: *Boyd Bennett* (King label): **$4,000**

David Bowie: *Diamond Dogs* (RCA label. Cover with visible canine genitals): **$4,000**

Jack Kerouac: *Poetry for the Beat Generation* (Hanover label): **$3,500**

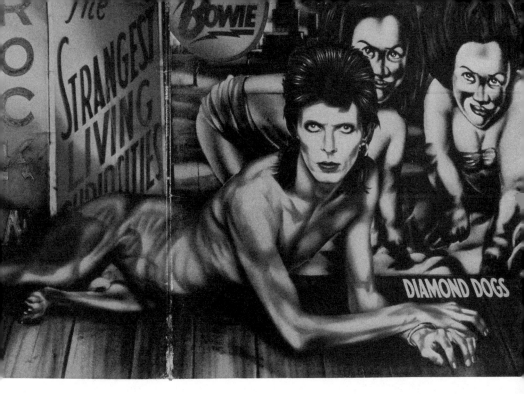

That was then, this is now. Close to 25 years later, those same records are valued as follows:

Bob Dylan: *The Freewheelin' Bob Dylan:* **$30,000** (stereo), **$12,000** (mono)

The Beatles: *The Beatles and Frank Ifield Onstage:* **$6,000**

The Beatles: *Introducing the Beatles:* **$12,000**

The Beatles: *Yesterday and Today: $12,000*

Ike & Tina Turner: *River Deep Mountain High* (Philles label): **$8,000**

Frank Ballard: *Rhythm-Blues Party* (Phillips Int'l label): **$5,000**

Boyd Bennett: *Boyd Bennett* (King label): **$4,000**

David Bowie: *Diamond Dogs* (RCA label. Cover with visible canine genitals): **$5,000**

Jack Kerouac: *Poetry for the Beat Generation* (Hanover label): **$10,000**

And thus we see, not *all* rare records consistently increase in value. Without getting into specific reasons, anything from a well conceived reissue taking the edge off demand for the original; through to supply-and-demand finding an equivocal level, can serve to depress a record's worth.

Or even (and this was especially common in the early years of Internet auctions), perhaps the "value" was set not by market forces *per se,* but by two or more collectors caught up in the thrill of the auction, and bidding not merely beyond the record's established value, but also beyond their rivals' pocketbook?

"Auction fever" is, after all, as well-established a phenomenon as any of the hobbies that it is capable of afflicting, driven not only by the desire to possess an item (for who knows when another might come along?), but also by sheer competitiveness.

Among the hobby's biggest hitters, however, it is rare for any to actually decline in value; and, once you move into the most rarified atmospheres of scarcity and value, another consideration comes into a play if the dollar signs *should* begin to falter.

Has a record stopped rising in price because nobody wants it any longer? Or because no further copies have appeared in the marketplace since the value was established?

There are a number of records listed in the price guides for which we might never see a rise in value, simply because only one copy exists and its owner is holding onto it.

Of these, the best known is the solitary acetate of the Quarrymen's (aka Paul McCartney, George Harrison and John Lennon) first recording together, a version of Buddy Holly's "That'll Be The Day," backed by McCartney and Harrison's original "In Spite of all the Danger." Pressed in 1958, McCartney owns the only existing copy and, while bootleg releases have rushed in to plug the gap in The Beatles collector's library, it is highly unlikely that this (admittedly not especially brilliant) record will ever see the business end of the auctioneer's hammer, at least during our lifetimes. Indeed, that single observation might well be the greatest

Released in 1964, *Introducing The Beatles* is a hit with collectors.

downside to building a collection purely for its investment value… even greater than being unable to actually *play* your records, for fear of reducing their value.

The fact remains that the only way to realize any profit that your hoarding has accumulated will be to physically part with your collection, and with it, all the joy and satisfaction that came from owning it in the first place.

There can be few people reading this, whatever their collecting passion, who do not still experience a pang of regret when remembering the records that they off-loaded on some now-distant day, and have been looking to replace ever since. Or *have* replaced, at a price at least commensurate with what they got for them in the first place.

Unless one is indeed a dyed-in-the-wool investor, with no more emotional connection to their collection than a banker to his stocks and bonds, it is safe to say that "future profit" is very much among the last things on a collector's mind.

Even in those rare moments of triumph when you find a $50 album for $1 in the bargain bin, and exultantly detail your triumph to any friends or family who will listen, actually *selling* the record is probably the last thing on your mind.

Owning it is reward enough; and, if you honor that ownership with the occasional gloating glance at its entry in the price guide, that too. Rare records should be celebrated *not* because they are worth a lot of money, but because they're difficult to obtain—which takes us back to the thrill of the hunt.

If a record is hard enough to find, it doesn't matter how much money you have to throw in its direction; it still won't appear.

"Rarity," after all, is a relative term. Is a record rare because a lot of people are looking for it, and there are a lot less copies available than there are prospective buyers? Or is it rare because there were very few pressed in the first place, and those few have already found safe homes?

The rarest record I own was released on the British Dawn label in 1972. For 40 years, I searched for a copy of *Been in the Pen Too Long*, the solo debut by former Mungo Jerry member Paul King, and in all that time I saw just two copies. The first belonged to a school friend who purchased it around the time of its release, and the second was delivered by the mailman just moments before these words were written.

The Internet was no help. Turning to the sites that are many collectors' first port of call, not a single copy has ever been traded on Discogs and only 10 have been logged by Popsike. To put that into perspective, that same site has seen over *200* copies of The Beatles' legendary butcher cover change hands in the same time span.

Does that mean this delightful slab of bluegrass pop rock is 20 times rarer than one of The Beatles' most storied treasures? Or that twenty times more people want, and can afford, The Beatles disc?

It doesn't matter. The fact is, if you want a butcher cover, all you need is cash. If you want Paul King, you are probably in for a very long wait.

If you've never heard of the Finnish band Punk Lurex OK, you won't care that there were only 500 copies pressed of their *1994-2003* compilation. But if you have, and you weren't one of the 500 who purchased it….

If Britain's Rikki and the Last Days of Earth don't float your boat, you wouldn't look twice at the lone 45 that a solo Rikki released in 1981, and the price guides don't care for it, either. But try and find a copy of it! Or its parent LP, for that matter.

And so on. Search for "the rarest records" online, and you will hear all about the established rarities of record collecting… the aforementioned Beatles' "butcher cover" and the first pressing of Bob Dylan's *Freewheeling;* the Sex Pistols single on A&M; John's Children's "Midsummer Night's Scene" 45; sundry Blue Note "deep groove" LPs; *etcetera.*

All fetch sums far in excess of what many collectors would (or even could) casually spend on a record. In terms of how many copies are actually out there, though, they're no *rarer* than any number of other records, and a lot more common than many others.

There's no more than a handful of copies known, for example, of TV Smith's Explorers' "Have Fun" 45, credited to front man Smith alone; and what

about promo copies of the Len Bright Combo's "Someone Must Have Nailed Us Together," issued not only with a press release but also a free nail!!??

To collectors of the artists in question, releases like these, and countless thousands more, are as precious as any megabuck Dylan or Elvis album, and probably required a lot more searching for, as well.

And that brings us to perhaps *the* single most important attribute any collector can gain—knowledge.

It's well known that David Bowie released a lot of records before he made it big, most of which are impossibly obscure. But only the truly devout might know, or even care, that the version of "Rebel Rebel" that RCA released as a promo 45 in spring 1974 features a completely different version of the song to the regular single or LP track—not just a different mix or an alternate take, but an entirely different arrangement and performance.

Most people know that mono pressings of The Beatles' albums featured different mixes to their stereo counterparts. But only Laura Nyro specialists would seek out Verve Folkways' mono pressing of the Divine Ms N's debut album, *More Than a New Discovery*, to hear it without all the ugly reverb slathered on by successive reissues.

And so it goes on. The first Neil Young album was still hot off the presses when Young took the tapes back and remixed four of the songs, before putting the new version out on the streets.

Jefferson Airplane's debut suffered a similar fate at the hands of their record company, after someone got cold feet about the inclusion of one song ("Running Round this World") and the lyrics of two others, "Let Me In" and "Run Around."

Fleetwood Mac's *Then Play On* was released in 1969 with a dozen tracks, including "When You Say" and "My Dream," then swiftly reissued with the hit "Oh Well" in their stead. The Rolling Stones's *Some Girls* had its jacket reworked after eagle-eyed lawyers realized they'd not received the necessary approval for the use of certain celebrities' faces. Early copies of the Partridge family's *Christmas Card* album arrived with a genuine Christmas card slotted into the front cover; later pressings either printed the card onto the sleeve, or went without it altogether.

A small quantity of Elvis Presley's *Aloha from Hawaii by Satellite* were utilized for an in-house promotion by the concert's TV sponsors, Van Camp; stickers featuring the company's Chicken of the Sea tuna, and a one-page promotional sheet mark out these very scarce discs.

None of these records are at all hard-to-find in their "regular" form; so much so that you have probably passed by dozens of copies as you flip through the contents of a record store rack.

But maybe you won't be so fast to do so in future.

Led Zeppelin released a self-titled box set in 1990. Supervised by Jimmy Page, the box set includes six vinyl records, 54 tracks and assorted other goodies.

Image courtesy Heritage Auctions

6

BOX SETS AND TREASURE TROVES

THE DEEPER INTO AN ARTIST'S career you travel, the more likely you are to find one. Or more.

Greatest Hits albums, after all, have been around, under one name or another, for as long as artists have been having hits. While less specific, and increasingly larger, anthologies were not far behind. And today? We are wearily (and, in financial terms, painfully) familiar today with the latter concept.

Box sets are the luxury items of the music industry.

Enter a well stocked store and you can almost literally hear the sturdiest shelves groaning beneath the weight of previously unreleased material, creaking behind hardbound coffee table books, awash with art prints and recycled memorabilia… fan club ephemera, reprinted press cuttings, buttons and plectrums and 8 x 10 photographs. Pink Floyd even gave away marbles and scarves with a couple of their boxes.

Entire albums are painstakingly documented from the scrappiest demo to the most shimmering surround sound remix; live material hitherto barely known to exist in listenable quality rings out in supersonic quality.

Fifty years after Bob Dylan toured in 1966, and his entire fan base had grown to love every muffled moment of the ensuing bootlegs, the *Live 1966* box unveiled no less than 23 of the shows (across 36 discs) in the greatest sound quality ever imagined.

Line that up alongside Pink Floyd's almost equally voluminous, and simultaneously released, *The Early Years* box of 10 CDs, nine DVDs, eight

Coming off the runaway success of their *Wish You Were Here* album, Pink Floyd's 1977 Animal tour was a spectacle of pyrotechnics, elaborate sets and the now-famous inflatable pigs.
Image courtesy Heritage Auctions

blu-rays and five re-pressed 45s, and one can scarcely imagine where the box set is destined to travel next.

Things were very different through the years when vinyl was *the* primary medium for music. Occasionally an enterprising major label might cobble together a collection of an artist's regular albums and box them up for a premium price—Queen, Pink Floyd and The Beatles are among the headliners to have received this treatment; periodically, a more specialist company might do much the same for a lesser-feted star—Sandy Denny and Nick Drake were early beneficiaries of this, with boxes that still catch the collector's eye.

The most familiar boxes, though, tended to be those produced by the likes of Reader's Digest, the Classics Record Library and the Book of the Month Club—sets that ranged from what now feel like very random selections of hits and oldies, through to more carefully curated studies of either an artist's entire career, or the highlights of a particular genre.

A 1981 BOMC box, for example, condensed 20 years of Judy Collins's career onto four LPs, complete with a delightfully produced booklet, just one in a series of very well-conceived collections that swung from classics and jazz to blues and Broadway.

Almost 20 years earlier, the Classics Record Library commenced production of a similarly grandiose series that again concentrated on classics, but they found room, too, for some remarkable folk-inflected collections: Four discs of *Folk Song and Minstrelsy* delved deep into the Vanguard Records archive to trace the roots of the folk boom that the likes of Collins (plus Dylan, Joan Baez and so many more) would ride to glory, and even took listeners to the most recent Newport Folk Festival to catch the best performers in their natural element.

Sets such as these are not especially hard to come by—indeed, they are more likely to be sighted in the local thrift store, or the dollar bins, than turning up in a dealer's advert in *Goldmine.* As forerunners of the modern box set, however, their place in collecting history is assured, and as anthologies in their own right, they are difficult to argue with.

The granddaddy of the modern box set, however, is a somewhat more conventional, and familiar, release. In 1985, as a prelude to Bob Dylan's still on-

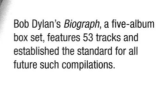

Bob Dylan's *Biograph*, a five-album box set, features 53 tracks and established the standard for all future such compilations.

going *Bootleg Series*, Columbia released *Biograph*, a five LP box that compiled familiar hit singles, favorite album tracks and a smattering of rarities across what Wikipedia proclaims to be "widely perceived as the first-ever box set."

Well, that's wrong, for a start. But still *Biograph* set the gold standard to which all future boxes needed to aspire, be they Led Zeppelin eponymous 1990 assemblage or, 25 years later, the solo Jimmy Page's *Soundtracks* collection; be it the first attempt to box up The Band's *Last Waltz* or *Woodstock*, or, again, the latest.

Across *Biograph*'s 53 tracks, no less than 18 performances were previously unreleased, and three more had only ever seen service on single. The collection did not fill every gap in the Dylan story (12-and-counting volumes of *The Bootleg Series* prove that), but it certainly whet the appetite for the delights that were to come as artists across the spectrum began

REINFORCE YOUR FOUNDATIONS: COLLECTIBLE VINYL BOX SETS

The Beatles: *10th Anniversary Box Set*
(Apple/Capitol—no cat #, 1974) current value:
$2,000

The Beatles: *Alpha Omega, Volume 1*
(Audio Tape Inc ATRBH 3583, 1972)
current value: **$50**

The Beatles: *Deluxe Box Set* (Capitol BBX1-
91302, 1988) current value: **$300**

Buddy Holly: *The Complete Buddy Holly*
(MCA 80000, 1981) current value: **$100**

David Bowie: *Sound + Vision* (Ryko Analogue
RALP 0120/1/2, 1989) current value: **$600**

Donovan: *A Gift from a Flower to a Garden*
(mono)(Epic L2N 6071, 1967) current value: **$175**

Ella Fitzgerald: *Sings the George and Ira
Gershwin Song Book* (Verve MGV-4029-5,
1959) current value: **$500**

Elvis Presley: *Elvis Aron Presley*
(RCA Victor CPL8-3699, 1980) current value: **$250**

Elvis Presley: *International Hotel, Las
Vegas Nevada, Presents Elvis, 1969*
(RCA no cat #, 1969) current value: **$3,000**

investigating their own deepest vaults.

In purely practical terms, the compact disc is the natural home for such packages. Much as fans might dream of a vinyl equivalent of, say, 1980s icons Dead Or Alive's 19 disc *Sophisticated Boom Box MMXVI* anthology (its release so cruelly coinciding with frontman Pete Burns' October 2016 passing), it would be impractical for all 220+ tracks to be released in a vinyl collection. Hence the decision to issue it instead as a seriously slimmed down 10 LP/80 songs collection, effectively reissuing the original albums that form the bedrock of the full feast.

Likewise, Dylan's aforementioned *Live 1966*, which spun off a vinyl release for just one of the concerts contained in the main package. While some remarkably hefty vinyl boxes have appeared in recent years (the

Zappa

Frank Zappa: *Joe's Garage, Acts 1, 2 and 3* (Barking Pumpkin 74206, 1986) current value: **$150**

Jack Kerouac: *The Jack Kerouac Collection* (Rhino R1-70939,1990) current value: **$120**

John Cage: *The 25-Year Retrospective Concert Of The Music Of John Cage* (no label/no cat, 1959) current value: **$300**

Led Zeppelin: *Led Zeppelin* (Atlantic 82144, 1990) current value: **$250**

Nick Drake: *Fruit Tree* (Hannibal HBNX 5302, 1986) current value: **$250**

Phil Spector: *Back to Mono 1958-1969* (Phil Spector/Abkco 7118-1, 1991) current value: **$120**

Various Artists: *The Artists and Music That Started It All* (Motown PR-84, 1981) current value: **$250**

Various Artists: *The Encyclopedia of Jazz on Records* (Decca DXF140, 1957) current value: **$275**

Various Artists: *The Motown Story: The First 25 Years* (Motown PR-121, 1983) current value: **$300**

Rolling Stones' *Mono Box* anthology of their entire 1960s output weighed in at a healthy 13 pounds), it seems that these box-set-lite editions are destined to be the new norm.

In collecting terms, as the above list proves, there's no doubt that Elvis rules the box set roost—thanks, largely, to a release that might not even be considered a box set in the first place. Rather, *International Hotel, Las Vegas Nevada, Presents Elvis, 1969* is essentially a box into which has been placed two regular albums and a heap of ephemera: a press release; a 1969 catalog; three photographs; and a thank-you note from Elvis and the Colonel. The value, of course, is in the box.

As for the perfect Elvis boxed set, there's no such animal. Short of being given a caseful of recordable CDs, and the keys to RCA's deepest vault, there's not an Elvis collector on earth who could be truly satisfied with what either the King's original label, the specialist Follow That Dream set-up, or a host of quasi-authorized others have offered up.

But that's not an indictment of the labels. It's an indication of just how personally people take these things. Collectors, most of all.

We want everything. Every time a new anthology appears, no matter how thorough it might be, or how specifically its remit is stated, there will always be people who will complain that something... a whole heap of somethings... isn't there.

When the Beatles' *In Mono* box was released in 2011, bringing together 11 albums worth of the band's original UK LPs, singles and b-sides, the die-hards complained that their US albums weren't included.

When the Rolling Stones offered a similar gesture five years later, but added the US albums too, people wanted to know why there were no out-takes added. But when the Stones *did* release an out-takes collection back in 1974, *Metamorphosis*, the moaners insisted that all the wrong songs had been included.

Because—we want everything. Even if it doesn't exist.

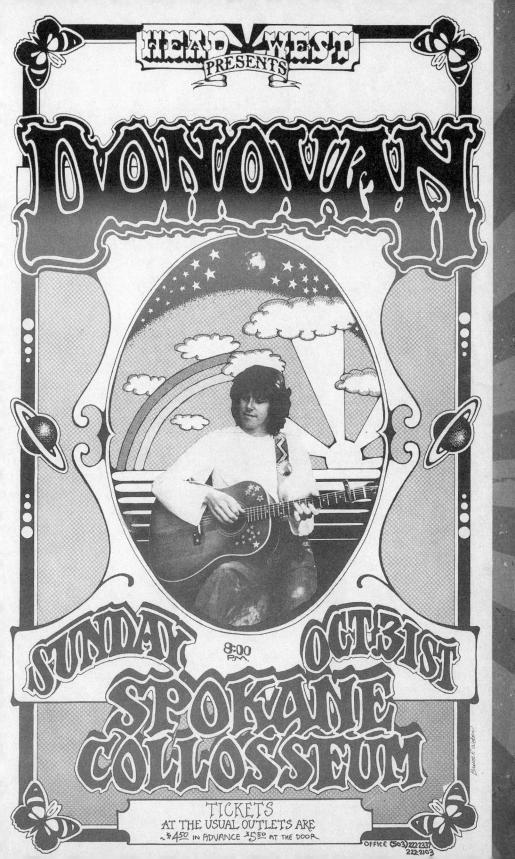

7

ALL THAT JAZZ

OF ALL THE COMMENTARIES THAT were heard and read as the latest, 2016, edition of the *Goldmine Jazz Album Price Guide* was being researched, one sentence in particular sticks in the mind: "A few years ago, you'd have struggled to give this record away. Now it's selling for...."

Collectors tastes change, cultural currents shift. They always have and they always will. Artists whom one generation ignored become heroes to the next; records once slighted become icons to the future.

In 1975, when Lou Reed released four sides of feedback and noise titled *Metal Machine Music*, his label could barely give copies away, so widely was

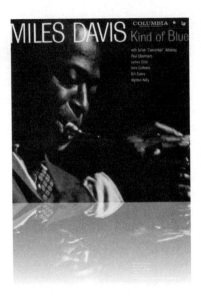 

it condemned. Today it is seen as an essential building block in the history of avant-garde music, and has been performed in the concert halls of the world by an orchestra.

Nowhere, however, has this process felt more pronounced than in the world of jazz. We are all familiar with the soaring values attached to the heaviest hitters of the jazz world—Blue Note and Prestige early pressings, Miles Davis and so forth.

But they are not the only batsmen on the field today. New generations make new discoveries. In 2004, in the second edition of the *Goldmine Jazz Album Price Guide*, Albert Ayler's *Spiritual Unity* (ESP-Disk 1002) LP was listed with a $25 value. Today, a near mint copy is rated close to forty times that amount. And that is by no means a solitary example.

Just 14 LPs are valued at $5,000 in the latest edition of the *Goldmine Standard Catalog of American Records*—that is, our listing of every album released in this country since 1950. Of these, just three are "regular" releases—that is, albums that were not, for whatever reason, withdrawn or even canceled before their official appearance. Two of those three are jazz albums: Sonny Clark's *Cool Struttin'* (Blue Note BLP-1588) and Jutta Hip's *With Zoot Sims* (Blue Note BLP-1530). (The third is the mono pressing of Jimi Hendrix's *Axis Bold As Love*, released just as the US industry abandoned mono for stereo).

Dip down a few notches. There are 139 albums priced at $1,000 in the full catalog. No less than 58 of them—that is, 42 percent—are jazz. Half that price and a similar ratio can again be found; of 337 LPs that list at $500, 134 are jazz records.

We should, of course, note that we are discussing records in the most uncommon of states—upwards of half-a-century old in many cases, and still looking and sound like new; Near Mint condition is as close as you can get to unplayed and unopened as it is possible to voyage, without coming upon a copy that has just left the pressing plant; and, needless to say, that is not something that a lot of original record buyers would ever have considered.

Records are made to be opened, records are made to be played, records are made to be enjoyed. They were the soundtracks to our lives, after all—in those days before radio and television, cassettes and mp3s, Internet streaming and laptop playlists transformed music into a commodity that sometimes feels no more precious than wallpaper, listening to records was tantamount to a sacred ritual, and one that would be indulged at every available moment.

Jazz was scarcely better served by the media of the day than any other genre outside of the easiest of easy listening—and less so, in fact, than

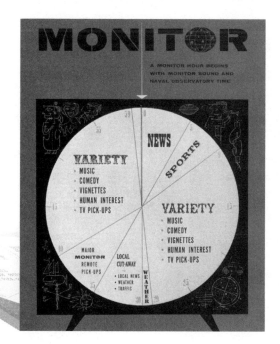

most. For many people listening in the 1950s, memories of the day seem to revolve around broadcasts of NBC's *Monitor*, debuting in 1955 as a weekends-only mix of chat, comedy, sport and interviews, but featuring a live jazz session from clubs around New York. The rest of the time, the fan was thrown back on his record collection. Or, at parties, on other peoples'.

The lack of airtime, of course contributed to the principle reason why many of these records are now so scarce. Even among the giants of the era, sales were low—so much so, in fact, that it was 1986 before any jazz album whatsoever was awarded a platinum disc (Herbie Hancock's *Future Shock*), while the Blue

Note label was forced to wait until 2001 before it received its first gold award for a jazz album, John Coltrane's *Blue Train*—most of whose sales were apparently racked up following its reissue on CD (BLP 1577). It remains the "classic era" Blue Note's sole million seller.

So, records got played, records got worn, records got scratched. Covers grew tatty. Inner bags were replaced. Even the most careful purchaser would eventually find age and use taking its toll. And yes, maybe if they'd had any idea of the future fortunes that were spinning on the turntable, they might at least have changed the stylus before it was dulled into a chisel.

But they didn't because who would? It is only over the last couple of decades that collectors have learned the lessons of the past, and become obsessed with keeping new purchases mint and poly-sleeved, and dealers in any of a hundred collecting disciplines can tell you what a waste of time and space (and polysleeves) that turned out to be.

Future rarities, after all, are seldom the items that everybody thinks they will be (and certainly not the ones that are marketed as such), and which they lock in the bank vault unopened. It's the ones that nobody bothers to save that turn out to be hardest to find.

But again, records are made to be opened, records are made to be played…. and the collecting market prices those "lesser" copies accordingly. Or it should—I still remember, after 20 years of searching, discovering one particular rarity at a record fair and, never having handled a copy before, let alone seen one priced so reasonably ($60, if I remember correctly, at a time when $600 was a more realistic cost), I removed it from its sleeve to inspect the vinyl. At which point, the dealer spoke.

"It's practically unplayed, VG+ at least." And he was right, it was. Apart from the great crack that ran from the outer edge to the spindle hole.

I replaced the record in the rack.

The point is, if you're a buyer, not to be discouraged by the highest prices that attend your wants list—and, while that is probably not the best story with which to illustrate this point, still the records you need are out there somewhere, affordably priced and playable too. And if they're not, or while you're awaiting their appearance, there are plenty more to be looking for.

You might want to hurry, though. As prices elsewhere throughout the jazz canon evidence (not to mention the remark with which we opened this introduction), the last few years have become very much a voyage of (re)discovery for many fans and collectors. Records that were, indeed, once impossible to give away have found voracious new audiences—a symbol not only of changing tastes, but also of changing times.

Artists whom past generations regarded as mere bandwagon jumpers (or worse) are constantly being re-evaluated by new audiences... the dollar or two for which their records might sell is a small price, after all, to pay for what might prove to be a great discovery, and social media ensures that word is not slow to spread.

We offer no examples—everybody reading this has probably passed such judgment on one artist or another. But from the meekest *jazz-lite* to the most unfused jazz fusion, audiences are eschewing the received wisdom of what is "good" and "bad" jazz, and simply having fun finding the sounds that match their own interpretations of those qualities.

Which, in turn, offers another indication of just how healthy the market for the music has become. People no longer want to hear only what they're told to listen to. They want to hear everything they can, and if they can be in on the ground floor of the next hero-in-waiting, all the better.

In 2004, the highest price listed for a Sun Ra album, 1968's *A Black Mass*, was $300, with others marked for as low as $40. Today, $300 is itself at the low end of the scale, and inflation alone is not wholly responsible for the increase in values.

Appreciation of, and interest in Sun Ra has also skyrocketed in the 21st century, not only from a purely musical point of view, but philosophically, too. An artist who once inhabited the outermost reaches of the popular consciousness has been accepted if not into the commercial mainstream, then at least its cultural equivalent. The already pronounced scarcity of his earliest (and, indeed, later) recordings became even sharper accordingly.

Similar tales abound as we delve deeper into the world of jazz, but one more will suffice, as we inspect the output of New York City's ESP-Disk label—home to the likes of the aforementioned Albert Ayler, Burton Greene, Karl Berger and Milton Graves. A dozen years ago, you could pick up more-or-less each artist's entire ESP-Disk catalog for less than you would today expect to pay for a single album.

No matter that few of the label's signings are in any way regarded as household names, even in the households where their records are collected. Like Blue Note, like Riverside, like Prestige and Savoy, ESP-Disk's very name has become known as a trademark of quality—an accolade that has never been a secret among its original supporters, of course. But which was certainly welcome news to anybody discovering

THE BIGGEST BUCKS—
TWENTY JAZZ HEAVY HITTERS

Amos Milburn: *Rockin' the Boogie* (Aladdin LP-704, 1952) current value: **$8,000**

Amos Milburn, Wynonie Harris &c: *Party After Hours* (Aladdin LP-703, 1952) current value: **$8,000**

Charles Brown: *Mood Music* (Aladdin LP-702, 1952) current value: **$7,500**

Dexter Gordon: *Gettin' Around* (Blue Note BLP-4204, 1965) current value: **$7,000**

Sonny Clark: *Cool Struttin'* (Blue Note BLP-1588, 1958) current value: **$5,000**

Jutta Hipp: *...with Zoot Sims* (Blue Note BLP-1530, 1956) current value: **$5,000**

John Coltrane: *Blue Train* (Blue Note BST-1577, 1957) current value: **$4,000**

Charlie Parker: *The Bird Blows the Blues* (Dial LP-901, 1949) current value: **$4,000**

Frank Sinatra: *Sinatra Jobim* (Reprise FS1028, 1969) current value: **$4,000**

the label in more recent years.

This upsurge of interest in artists, labels and even sub-genres who might once have been considered cultish, even "marginal," is not a phenomenon that is unique to jazz.

Across the musical spectrum, the last decade or so has seen any number of once forgotten (or at least, generally overlooked) figures elevated to a degree of popular acclaim, whether by a piece of music well-placed within a television commercial or popular drama, or simply through word-of-mouth—again, the impact of social media cannot be overlooked whenever one encounters a sudden surge in some hitherto unknown artist's popularity.

Jazz just seems to have a lot of artists who fit the billing.

Also playing a significant role has been the recent rush of CD box sets gathering together both the rarest, and the best known, of a given artist's catalog—often at prices that could easily compete with a more-or-less

Tina Brooks: *Back to the Tracks* (Blue Note BLP-4052, 1960)
current value: **$3,500**

Sonny Clark: *Dial "S" for Sonny* (Blue Note BLP-1570, 1957)
current value: **$3,500**

Kenny Dorham: *...Octet/Sextet* (Blue Note BLP-1535, 1963)
current value: **$3,500**

Lee Morgan: *City Lights* (Blue Note BLP-1575, 1958) current value: **$3,500**

Tommy Flanagan: *Overseas* (Prestige PRLP-7134, 1958) current value: **$3,500**

Curtis Fuller: *The Opener* (Blue Note BLP-1567, 1957) current value: **$3,000**

Dexter Gordon: *Dexter Blows Hot and Cool* (Dootone DL-207, 1956)
current value: **$3,000**

Charlie Parker: *Charlie Parker* (Dial LP-203, 1949) current value: **$2,500**

Art Pepper: *Modern Art* (Intro 606, 1957) 206 value: **$2,500**

Sonny Rollins: *Saxophone Colossus* (Prestige PRLP-7079, 1957)
current value: **$2,500**

Sun Ra: *Jazz by Sun Ra* (Transition TLP-10, 1957) current value: **$2,500**

complete collection of the same music on LP. The curious buy the box set. The converts pick up the vinyl.

Indeed, another factor is the much-vaunted, and much-welcomed, rebirth of vinyl on the new release racks. In March 2016, industry news sources reported that, for the first time ever, vinyl revenues had not only eclipsed those raked in by the ad-supported music streaming sites, but were closing in on subscriber-funded services, too.

To this can be added a massive 52.1% rise in vinyl revenues in just the past year, compared to a 32.5% *decline* in CDs, and still one is seeing only a fraction of the overall picture.

For used record sales, too, are booming, not only in terms of individual values but also across the board, from the most humble dollar box to the most exclusive rarities. And this book celebrates that fact.

Collecting has never, after all, been purely a matter of simply joining the dots in an artist's discography, and counting down the days until the collection is "complete." It has always been a voyage of discovery, a journey into musical unknowns that are as labyrinthine as your curiosity allows them to be.

That sentiment just feels more applicable to jazz than to any other genre.

The great jazz saxophonist Dexter Gordon photographed by Herman Leonard.
Image courtesy Heritage Auctions

R.P.I. Field House TROY, N.Y.

1 Show Only Tuesday May 6 8:30 P.M.

All seats reserved. $1.50, 2.00, 2.50, 3.00 All tax exempt. Tickets on sale now: Field House
Frear's Dept. Store, Troy. Ten Eyck Record Store & Blue Note Shop, Albany.
Apex Record Korner, Schenectady.

TOP ATTRACTIONS
4 GREAT BANDS
Cast of 60

17 TOP ATTRACT
4 Great BAN
60 STARS

ALL IN PERSON SHOW

ALL IN PERSON S

ALAN FREED presents THE

BIG BEAT

JERRY LEE LEWIS & BAND
"BREATHLESS"
"GREAT BALLS OF FIRE"

☆ BUDDY HOLLY
"I'M GOING TO LOVE YOU TOO"
"PEGGY SUE"

☆ The CRICKETS
"MAYBE, BABY" — "OH BOY"

☆ CHUCK BERRY
"SWEET LITTLE 16" - "ROCK n ROLL MUSIC"

☆ FRANKIE LYMON
"THUMB, THUMB"

☆ THE DIAMONDS
"THE STROLL"

DANNY AND THE JUNIORS
"AT THE HOP" - "ROCK 'N ROLL IS HERE TO STAY"

☆ BILLY & LILLIE
"LA DEE DAH"

☆ Billy FORD AND THE THUNDERBIRD

★ The CHANTELS
"MAYBE"

Larry WILLIAMS & ORCH
"BONY MORONIE"

The PASTELS
"BEEN SO LONG"

ALAN FREED and his CORAL RECORDS
BIG ROCKING BAND
★ Starring SAM The MAN TAYLOR
New Hit! "BIG GUITAR"

★ DICKY DOO and the DONT'S
"CLICK-CLACK"

★ SCREAMIN' Jay HAWKIN
"I PUT A SPELL ON YOU"

★ JO ANN CAMPBE
"WAIT A MINUTE"

ED TOWNSEND "For You Love"

CHAPTER 8

THE BIRTH OF ROCK 'N' ROLL

THE HISTORY OF POPULAR MUSIC is not linear, a simple case of traveling from point A (the beginning) to point Z (today). Rather, it is a succession of musical genres that rise and fall, dominating and shifting the hitherto prevalent moods of the day but then, once absorbed into the mainstream, fading into the background, a constant presence but no longer a driving force.

Collectors, however, remember and, if they are so inclined, they collect. They also argue. When did their chosen genre begin? When did it end? Which artists truly espoused its driving passions, and which ones merely jumped aboard an already rolling bandwagon?

There are no answers to these questions; or, there are, but there are as many answers as there are people to ask the questions in the first place; and nowhere is the argument so pronounced as the one that asks what was the first rock 'n' roll record ever released.

The list of candidates is certainly impressive: "That's All Right, Mama" by Arthur "Big Boy" Crudup (1946); "Good Rockin' Tonight" by Wynonie Harris (1948); "Rock This Joint" by Jimmy Preston and his Prestonians (1949); "Saturday Night Fish Fry" by Louis Jordan & The Tympany Five

This 1958 concert handbill, featuring Buddy Holly, Jerry Lee Lewis and legendary DJ Alan Freed, epitomizes the classic era of 1950s rock 'n' roll.
Image courtesy Heritage Auctions

(1949) and "Rocket 88" by Jackie Brenston and his Delta Cats (better known as Ike Turner and the Kings of Rhythm, 1951) can all stake a claim.

In terms of the general public, however, the kids who poured out in their droves to buy the "new" music, and the parents who rose up in even greater numbers to condemn it, rock 'n' roll began with Bill Haley and the Comets' "Rock Around the Clock," the title theme to the movie of the same name.

The song itself was already a couple of years old; it was written in 1952 by Max C. Freedman and Jimmy De Knight (aka James E. Myers), and had already been recorded by Sonny Dae and His Knights.

Neither was the sound especially fresh—Haley and his Comets had cut a very similar record in 1953, "Crazy Man Crazy."

But "Rock Around the Clock" was the record that the fates determined would kick start rock 'n' roll, storming to the top of the *Billboard* charts, and suddenly the hills were alive with this new demon beat. Little Richard, Jerry Lee Lewis, Gene Vincent, Chuck Berry, Eddie Cochran, Buddy Holly, Elvis Presley all emerged, and many more besides.

Some were already veteran performers, either adopting the new beat (or being adopted by it); others made their debut with the rock 'n' roll sound. It didn't matter. Rock 'n' roll, as the song insisted, was here to stay.

That story is well known, of course. What is frequently less remarked upon is the medium in which most early rock fans bought their records. Not on the long established 78 rpm discs, but on the new-fangled 45s. True, 78s would remain the dominant format in the marketplace for another few years, but sales of 45s were catching up every year, and it was rock 'n' roll that led the charge – a new medium for a new music.

Of course, many collectors do pursue the early

Bill Haley and the Comets circa 1950s.
Image courtesy Heritage Auctions.

"That's All Right," one of the original Elvis Presley releases on Sun Records.

"IN TERMS OF LEGEND, RARITY AND (MORE SUBJECTIVELY) QUALITY, **ELVIS PRESLEY** TOPS THE ROCK 'N' ROLL 45S CHART, OF COURSE."

rockers on 78. The prices might be higher and the search more complicated. It's not so easy to "cheat," or be misled, and pick up a later repressing or reissue in lieu of a particularly hard to find item. It's a rewarding, if time and cash-consuming hobby.

But somehow, 45s *feel* more authentic; more in tune with rock 'n' roll's rebellious nature, sweeping way the sounds and attitudes of the past and opening the world up to a whole new beat. We saw in an earlier chapter how RCA, manufacturers of the first 45s, invoked the "teenager" as the primary market for the new format. Rock 'n' roll confirmed that because it, too, was targeted at teens.

Forming a rock 'n' roll collection is as easy or as hard as you want it to be, no matter where or when you choose to begin your hunt. Remember, the original 45s that you are probably chasing are now all more-or-less 60 years old, and a lot can happen to a piece of plastic in that time.

Even the biggest and best-selling hit singles are difficult to track down in more than roughly playable condition, while lesser successes are likely to prove even more elusive. But they're out there, and if they're not, the reissue market overflows with later

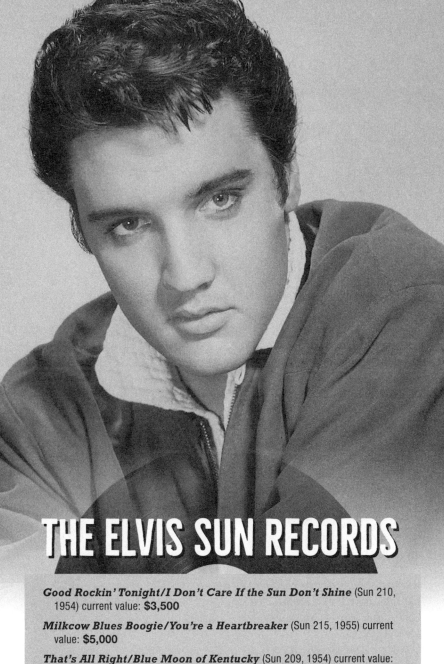

Image courtesy Heritage Auctions.

THE ELVIS SUN RECORDS

Good Rockin' Tonight/I Don't Care If the Sun Don't Shine (Sun 210, 1954) current value: **$3,500**

Milkcow Blues Boogie/You're a Heartbreaker (Sun 215, 1955) current value: **$5,000**

That's All Right/Blue Moon of Kentucky (Sun 209, 1954) current value: **$10,000**

Baby Let's Play House/I'm Left, You're Right, She's Gone (Sun 217, 1955) current value: **$3,000**

I Forgot to Remember to Forget/Mystery Train (Sun 223, 1955) current value: **$2,500**

pressings. Collect the labels, collect the songs, collect them however you wish. Just do it.

In terms of legend, rarity and (more subjectively) quality, Elvis Presley tops the rock 'n' roll 45s chart, of course. Particularly when you consider what he was getting up to before fame came a-knocking.

He released five singles for Sam Phillips' Sun label before moving to RCA and becoming a superstar, and all five rate high in any poll of rarities:

And yes, all five have since been reissued on a number of occasions, but they carry the RCA label. The Sun originals are as scarce as they are legendary.

But Sun itself is not overall a difficult label to collect.

Jerry Lee Lewis, for example, enjoyed a far longer, and much more prolific stay with Sun than

The Killer, Jerry Lee Lewis in a promotional photo
for *Jamboree*, a 1957 feature from Warner Bros.

Elvis, during which he too delivered several of his signature hits. But his label discography is less sought-after and, correspondingly, easier to gather up, even if you only focus on the early years.

Crazy Arms/End of the Road (Sun 259, 1957) current value: **$125**

Whole Lot of Shakin' Going On/It'll Be Me (Sun 267, 1957)
current value: **$50**

Great Balls of Fire/You Win Again (Sun 281, 1957) current value: **$100**

Breathless/Down the Line (Sun 288, 1958) current value: **$50**

High School Confidential/Fools Like Me (Sun 296, 1958)
current value: **$100**

Lewis Boogie/The Return of Jerry Lee (Sun 301, 1958) current value: **$40**

I'll Make It All Up to You/Break-Up (Sun 303, 1958) current value: **$40**

I'll Sail My Ship Alone/It Hurt Me So (Sun 312, 1958) current value: **$30**

Lovin' Up a Storm/Big Blon' Baby (Sun 317, 1959) current value: **$30**

Let's Talk About Us/Ballad of Billy Joe (Sun 324, 1959) current value: **$30**

Little Queenie/I Could Never Be Ashamed of You (Sun 330, 1959)
current value: **$30**

Old Black Joe/Baby Baby, Bye Bye (Sun 337, 1960) current value: **$30**

Hang Up My Rock and Roll Shoes/John Henry (Sun 344, 1960)
current value: **$30**

And, fortunately for the majority of collectors, the vast majority of early rock 'n' roll 45s do fall closer in price to the Jerry Lee standards than to Elvis on Sun—indeed, just a few months later, with Presley now racking up the hits on RCA, we see his own high values take a considerable dive. And that includes the earliest of the aforementioned Sun reissues.

I Forgot to Remember to Forget/Mystery Train (RCA Victor 47-6357, 1955)
current value: **$70**

That's All Right/Blue Moon of Kentucky (RCA Victor 47-6380, 1955)
current value: **$70**

Good Rockin' Tonight/I Don't Care If the Sun Don't Shine (RCA Victor
47-6381, 1955) current value: **$70**

Milkcow Blues Boogie/You're a Heartbreaker (RCA Victor 47-6382, 1955)
current value: **$70**

Baby Let's Play House/I'm Left, You're Right, She's Gone (RCA Victor
47-6383, 1955) current value: **$70**

Rebel rocker Gene Vincent influenced many future artists, including a young Paul McCartney.
Image Courtesy Heritage Auctions.

Of course, there is so much more to collecting vintage rock 'n' roll than Elvis, Jerry Lee or Sun. Although albums were scarcely regarded with the same awe as 45s, by either industry or consumers, many of the era's greatest artists released now-collectible (and often excellent) long-players—although just as many did not, until either tragedy or nostalgia drew the first compilations out of the vault.

Of the era's most collected album artists, we have already established that Elvis is streets ahead. But Gene Vincent is very close behind him. For at his peak, brief though it was, Gene Vincent was rebellion personified. And rebellion, of course, is what great rock 'n' roll is all about.

Crippled in a motorcycle accident during his days in the U.S. Navy, Vincent Eugene Craddock wrote what became his signature hit, "Be-Bop-A-Lula," while recuperating in Portsmouth Navy Hospital in early 1956. A couple of years later, it would be the first record a young Paul McCartney ever bought.

10 GREAT ROCK 'N' ROLL SINGLES

Big Bopper: *Chantilly Lace/The Purple People Eater Meets the Witch Doctor* (Mercury 71343, 1958) current value: **$30**

Bo Diddley: *Bo Diddley/I'm a Man* (Checker 814, 1955) current value: **$60**

Buddy Holly: *Peggy Sue/Everyday* (Coral 61885, 1957) current value: **$60**

Carl Perkins: *Blue Suede Shoes/Honey Don't* (Sun 234, 1956) current value: **$70**

Chuck Berry: *Roll Over Beethoven/Drifting Heart* (Chess1626, 1956) current value: **$60**

Eddie Cochran: *Summertime Blues/Live Again* (Liberty55144, 1958) current value: **$40**

Elvis Presley: *Heartbreak Hotel/I Was the One* (RCA Victor 47-6420, 1956) current value: **$50**

Fats Domino: *Blueberry Hill/Honey Chile* (Imperial X5407, 1956) current value: **$30**

Gene Vincent: *Be-Bop-a-Lula/Woman Love* (Capitol F3450, 1956) current value: **$75**

Ritchie Havens: *Donna/La Bamba* (Del-Fi4110, 1958) current value: **$75**

Released from hospital and the service, dragging his damaged left leg behind him, Vincent turned his attention to the newly emergent rock 'n' roll. He formed a band, the Blue Caps (named for President Eisenhower's golfing headgear), and began playing around town.

The band's sound was primitive, raw, and excitement personified... or so Bill "Sheriff Tex" Davis, a DJ at the local W.C.M.S. country radio station, thought. Vincent and the band played a couple of the station's Country Showtime broadcasts before Davis took them into the studio to record three songs: Vincent's own "Be-Bop-A-Lula" and "Race With The Devil" included.

It was the era of the Svengali manager, and Davis—as firm an admirer of Colonel Tom Parker as Vincent was a Presley fan— knew exactly what he needed to do. Buying a co-writing credit for "Be-Bop-A-Lula" from Vincent (it cost him $25, money well spent whatever the song's eventual fate),

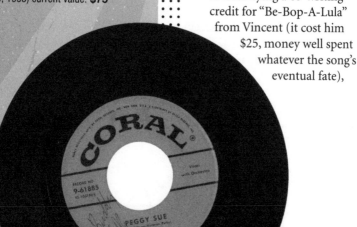

Davis then approached Capitol Records producer Ken Nelson with a copy of the tape.

Nelson pounced. Capitol, together with every other record label in the land, was currently locked into a desperate search for the next Elvis, and Vincent's almost spot-on recreation of the King was music to the label's ears.

On May 4 1956, the Blue Caps were taken to Nashville's Owen Bradley Studios, where they reprised "Be-Bop-A-Lula" and "Race With The Devil," banged out a soaring "I Still Miss You," and then threw in a brooding version of Jack Rhodes' "Woman Love." By the end of the day, Gene Vincent and the Blue Caps were Capitol Records artists. Capitol had their Elvis, and if anybody doubted the fact, they only had to ask Presley's own band mate Bill Black.

One evening, Black, Presley and Scotty Moore were driving to a gig when Vincent came on the radio. Black immediately accused Presley of going behind his band's back and making records for another label, and he wouldn't be dissuaded, no matter how much Presley denied it.

Capitol, of course, would be keen to keep a rumor like that in circulation for as long as they could; besides, to the corporate bigwigs, one rock 'n' roller was much the same as another, and what was Vincent anyway, but another two-bit kid who could sing a little? It didn't take them long, however, to realize that there was an exception to every rule... and they'd signed it.

Uncooperative, surly, a heavy drinker, Vincent refused to tow the company line on anything, and just when Capitol figured things couldn't get any worse... they did. Ken Nelson had decided "Woman Love" should be Vincent's first single, and with good reason. It was a great performance, a moody slice of lascivious rockabilly that had more than a hint of Elvis around its delivery. Unfortunately, it was also one Vincent would have preferred to see buried away on the B-side, instead of his own "Be-Bop-A-Lula."

Absolutely unwilling to chance a self-composed debut for their new sensation, Capitol stuck their ground, right up until the first promos went out, and every DJ in the land flipped the record over. And while it is true that many of them considered "Woman Love" way too racy for contemporary radio (the song was actually banned by Britain's BBC), that wasn't the only reason they rejected it. The real reason was, "Be-Bop-A-Lula" was better. By mid-June, the hastily revised 45 had entered the chart. By early August, "Be-Bop-A-Lula" was No. 7.

The Blue Caps were back in the studio almost immediately, cutting a B-side ("Gonna Back Up Baby") for their next single, "Race With The Devil," before getting down to their debut album. Delighted though he was with "Be-Bop-A-Lula," however, producer Ken Nelson wasn't at all certain

The classic *Bluejean Bop!* by Gene Vincent and his Blue Caps.

that the Blue Caps were good enough to record a full album. When the band arrived at the studio, then, they were greeted by a handful of session musicians, just waiting to pounce upon the first sign of inexperience.

The Blue Caps blew them away; by the end of the first session, the group had undisputed mastery of the studio, and over the next three days, they slammed 16 songs onto tape, enough for an album and a few B-sides besides.

Bluejean Bop! is as schizophrenic as any album of its era, serving up more than its fair share of reasonably rocked up old pop classics, alongside the meat and potatoes of Vincent's preferred repertoire. But it was that meat and potatoes which mattered, ensuring that at least half of *Bluejean Bop!* remains one of the most solid, and solidly realized collections of the entire era, a classic of deliciously debauched rockabilly, and the prototype not only for the remainder of Vincent's career, but for every rockabilly act which has followed him.

Indeed, "Bluejean Bop!" itself, pulled off the album as a 45 after "Race With The Devil" signally failed to emulate its predecessor, ranks amongst the most potent statements of intent any single musician has ever accomplished, pounding insistence shot through with a guitar line which wanders all across the musical spectrum, without ever losing sight of the business in hand.

It is difficult today to judge precisely what a splash Vincent made. Even his most diehard admirers admit that he was at his best in person, either onstage or on the screen, where the full impact of his physical appearance hit the eyes with the same intensity as his music assaulted the ears.

Hair uncombed, skinny frame cloaked in blue jeans and leather jacket, he used his disability as a weapon, contorting his body painfully around that useless limb, screwing up his face as he sang, scruffy, disheveled, a guy from so far across the wrong side of the tracks that there was no coming home once you got there.

And his songs! He conjured a world where the dancers had crazy legs, and everything was wrapped up in blue jeans; where John got slapped and honeys jumped back, where cats and kittens consorted every night, but most of all... worst of all... it was a world where "Bop Street" was the center of the universe, a smoky hole of disrepute, all slinky guitars and sexy girls, and the jukebox pounded rock all night.

By the time Vincent and Blue Caps made their big screen debut in Jayne Mansfield's *The Girl Can't Help It* movie, their reputation had already ensured their notoriety, and a repeat airing for "Be-Bop-A-Lula" did the rest.

The band started work on its second album in October, but Vincent remained a problem. Attempts to soften the singer's style by bringing the Jordanaires into the studio were met with such indifference that nobody was surprised when the first single from the 15 song sessions, the heavily Presley-fied "Important Words," sank without trace, in January, 1957; nor that nothing else from the album had a chance of remedying that situation.

Still, "Cat Man," "Cruisin'," "Hold Me, Hug Me, Rock Me" and "Double Talkin' Baby" at least conformed to Vincent's established musical persona; a version of "Unchained Melody" proved that he had an eye for the unexpected; while "Red Blue Jeans And A Ponytail" so successfully distilled Vincent's essence that it almost sounds like a parody!

The overall disappointment of the band's sophomore album was reflected in its sales; Vincent, however, could still kick hard when he felt like it, and in March, "Bi-I-Bickey-Bi, Bo-Bo-Go" was unleashed as a truly dynamic 45. Its undeniable chances of chart success, however, were stymied first, when Vincent found himself caught in the middle of a major battle between a group of rival booking agents, and was unable to tour; then when manager Davis resigned, rather than try to untangle the situation.

Never blessed with a stable line-up, the Blue Caps were unraveling, and so was Vincent's health. The constant touring had wreaked havoc on his leg, and finally, in June 1957, the singer decided to listen to both his doctors and his record company mentors. While the former encased his leg in the metal brace he would wear for the remainder of his life, Vincent placed his career in the hands of Sonny James' manager, Ed McLemore, Vincent prepared to embrace musical maturity.

Across a two-day session, June 19/20, 1957, a new single was recorded which would completely tear up Vincent's musical form book, a powerful, but distinctly harmless reading of "Lotta Lovin'," backed by an almost cloyingly over-arranged version of Bobby Darin/Don Kirschner's "Wear My Ring." It became his biggest hit since "Be-Bop-A-Lula," and sensing that this was, indeed, what his audience now wanted, Vincent prepared to give them more of the same.

A frenzied rocker, but again somehow emasculated by the fuller sound, and country-tinged guitars which the latest Blue Caps line-up so effortlessly created, "Dance To The Bop" climbed to #23, ten places below "Lotta Love," but still high enough for a third album to be called for, *Gene Vincent Rocks And The Blue Caps Roll*.

Undeniably, the sound was softening even further... too far for some people's tastes, in fact, as both a new single, "I Got A Baby," and the album itself sold badly. Another single from the sessions, "Baby Blue," fared no better, and again Vincent's career was taking a downward turn.

He landed a part in the juvenile delinquency movie *Hot Rod Gang*, and would be cutting a soundtrack E.P. to accompany it, but to no avail. Now, drinking heavily, taking painkillers both for his leg and for fun, Vincent insisted on returning to the road, one desperate, last ditch attempt to recapture his early momentum.

Vincent often shared a bill with rising star Eddie Cochran, igniting a friendship that would survive the remainder of Cochran's short life; headlining the weeklong Rock And Roll Jubilee Of Stars, in Philadelphia, the pair became a virtual double act, and from thereon in, they were all but inseparable. Cochran's imprimatur is all over September 1958's *A Gene Vincent Record Date With The Blue Caps* album; his was the first voice you heard on the "Git It" single.

But still that elusive successor to "Dance To The Bop" remained far out of sight. Later in the year, "Say Mama" became the Blue Caps' final single; the *Sounds Like Gene Vincent* album, their last will and testament.

Midway through their latest tour, in late 1958, Vincent disbanded the group. They hadn't been paid in three weeks, and the Musicians Union was threatening him with suspension (his union card would, in fact, be withheld for a short time). It had been a year since his last hit, and he had a new wife, Darlene Hicks, to support. Abandoning L.A., Vincent fled for the wilds of Washington State, and began gigging with whichever local musicians came to hand.

One of these was guitarist Jerry Merritt, and in June, 1959, with the Yakima native firmly established as his right hand man, Vincent set off on one of the first rock 'n' roll tours of Japan, a spectacularly successful outing which played to over a quarter of a million rabid fans in less than a week.

Vincent, however, never took to the country, and actually flew home early, leaving a leaderless band still facing a handful more shows. There was, Merritt decided, only one thing they could do. *He* would be Gene Vincent! "I shouldn't have done it, I guess," he admitted later. "But nobody suspected anything, and it was just one of those wild things you'd get into when you were around Gene Vincent!"

Merritt returned to the

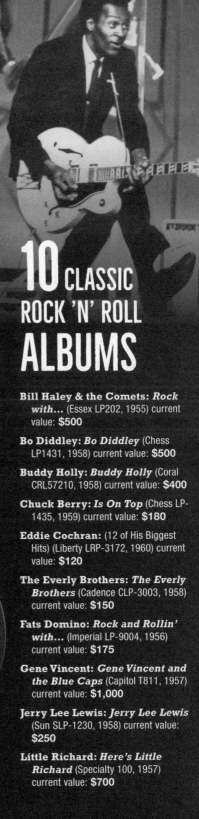

10 CLASSIC ROCK 'N' ROLL ALBUMS

Bill Haley & the Comets: *Rock with...* (Essex LP202, 1955) current value: **$500**

Bo Diddley: *Bo Diddley* (Chess LP1431, 1958) current value: **$500**

Buddy Holly: *Buddy Holly* (Coral CRL57210, 1958) current value: **$400**

Chuck Berry: *Is On Top* (Chess LP-1435, 1959) current value: **$180**

Eddie Cochran: (12 of His Biggest Hits) (Liberty LRP-3172, 1960) current value: **$120**

The Everly Brothers: *The Everly Brothers* (Cadence CLP-3003, 1958) current value: **$150**

Fats Domino: *Rock and Rollin' with...* (Imperial LP-9004, 1956) current value: **$175**

Gene Vincent: *Gene Vincent and the Blue Caps* (Capitol T811, 1957) current value: **$1,000**

Jerry Lee Lewis: *Jerry Lee Lewis* (Sun SLP-1230, 1958) current value: **$250**

Little Richard: *Here's Little Richard* (Specialty 100, 1957) current value: **$700**

Touring together, Eddie Cochran and a black-leathered Gene Vincent.

U.S. in time to join drummer Sandy Nelson and bassist Red Callender in the studio, where Vincent was set to record his sixth album, *Crazy Times*.

It was, by the singer's recent standards, a strong record, with Merritt's "She She Sheila," Don Covay's "Big Fat Saturday Night," and a tremendous cover of "Ac-Cent-Tchu-Ate The Positive" all crying out for recognition. But it sold poorly and by the time Vincent received an invitation to tour Britain in late 1959, he had all but accepted that his career in America was at an end.

Britain, however, was a different matter entirely. On December 5,

1959, Vincent arrived in London for some surprise guest appearances on homegrown sensation Marty Wilde's latest tour, backed by a ready-made English band, Colin Green and the Beat Boys—future Shadows Brian Bennett and Licorice Locking, and keyboard player Georgie Fame. His first date, however, was on the set of wildcat rock 'n' roll television producer Jack Good's *Boy Meets Girl*. And the modern legend of Gene Vincent started right there.

For all his menace and malice and bad reputation, Gene Vincent had been extraordinary only in his stance and scruffiness; it was the perception of evil which horrified people, not only physical sense of it. What Good wanted to do was extend that perception to its furthest boundaries, to make Gene Vincent look as horrific as the world's moms and pops already thought he was.

Off came the jeans, and the shirts and the hats; off came any resemblance to an even halfway respectable human being. When Vincent rolled out onto the *Boy Meets Girl* set, he was a demon dipped in tight black leather, twisting his body beneath a single white spotlight, barely moving, never smiling, just sweating and smoking and oozing through his outfit, while a pick-up band, the Firing Squad, ground its way through steamy versions of "Rocky Road Blues," "Frankie And Johnny," "Wild Cat" and "Right Here On Earth."

Good couldn't have molded anything if it wasn't there to begin with, but by the time Vincent set foot back on stage, touring the UK alongside, again, Eddie Cochran, the mutation was complete. Cochran was every cocky teenager's dream come true; Vincent was every outcast's idol. Together on the same concert bill, they reached out to every rock 'n' roll fan in the land.

And then Cochran died, killed in a car crash as he headed back to London for a red-eye flight to L.A. at the end of the first leg of the tour, on April 17, 1960. Vincent was in the car with him, but while he emerged from the wreck physically unscathed, emotionally he would never recover. His career would continue with both good records and bad, and when he died on October 12, 1971, not one of the tributes to his life and career could be accused to having been hyperbolic. At his best, Vincent really was everything that rock 'n' roll should be.

And if you really want to start collecting the genre, Gene Vincent is where you might consider beginning.

A 21-year-old Elvis Presley earned the nickname "Elvis the Pelvis" in part to his gyrating performance on *The Milton Berle Show* in 1956.
Bettman/Getty Images

CHAPTER 9

AND THEN THERE WAS ELVIS

IN TERMS OF MODERN RECORD collecting, Elvis Presley is Year One. People collected records before Elvis came along and a lot of earlier records (and artists) are very collectible: Frank Sinatra, for example; Bing Crosby; Roy Rogers et al. But Elvis' records weren't simply collected; they were hoarded on an industrial scale, a phenomenon that began almost as soon as he scored his first hit.

Certainly his record label, RCA, saw the way the wind was blowing; the wholesale reissue of Elvis' first five singles, originally released by Sun Records, demonstrates that. So does the decision to release an album titled *For LP Fans Only*, at a time when singles (and extended play EPs) were the pocket-money purchase of choice. For a lot of people, that was the first LP they ever bought, but it would not be the last.

Bearing in mind the sheer number of Elvis Presley records sold over the years—almost 140 million in the U.S. alone, including 90 gold albums, 53 platinum and 25 multi-platinum—collecting Elvis does not need to be an especially costly pursuit.

Of course he has more than his share of solid-gold rarities, with that first run of Sun label 45s close to the top of every fan's wants list. But when a CD box set featuring every one of the albums he released throughout his lifetime was released in 2016, more than one fan took that as a challenge, to forgo the easy option of purchasing the box, and instead hunting down those same LPs in their original vinyl state. With a laissez-faire attitude toward condition, early pressings and the other minutiae of hard-core collecting, the dollar bins of America could yield up almost every disc on the want list, at half the price of the compact discs.

Such an approach is satisfying from the point of view of simply crossing things off the want list. But, of course, there is a great deal more to collecting than that, and the world of Elvis vinyl offers perhaps more opportunities for specialization than any artist outside of The Beatles.

Original mono, stereo, quad and electronically-processed pressings,

ELVIS SUN RECORDS

The toughest task for an Elvis collector is to find the King's Sun Records 45s. Reproductions of the Sun records abound, with some of the reproductions actually featuring out-of-stock Sun labels.

Any Elvis Sun recording pressed on colored or swirled vinyl is a reproduction: originals were pressed only in black. There were never any "picture sleeves" for Elvis Sun recordings, either. And Sun never made any four-song EPs of Elvis' songs, so any that you find are phonies.

Of Presley's five Sun releases, legitimate copies of his first four releases have "push marks" – three circles pressed into the label itself. Not all the originals have push marks, but because the collectible value of a Sun 45 is extremely high, and since so many counterfeit and reproduced Sun 45s exist because of this, collectors look for the "push marks" to confirm a true Memphis pressing.

Presley's fifth Sun release, "Mystery Train"/"I Forgot to Remember to Forget" (Sun 223) does not contain push marks on the label. If the record has a triangle in the dead wax it was pressed by Monarch Record Pressing in Los Angeles.

After Sam Phillips sold Elvis' contract to

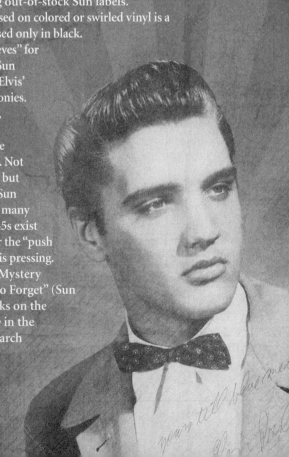

early (and earliest) pressings, sleeve and label variations, inner bags, even the stickers affixed to the original record sleeves, have all been ruthlessly cataloged and compiled—indeed, the aforementioned CD box set certainly won plaudits for its attention to detail via the inclusion of a sheet of stickers, replicating those found on original LP releases.

These avenues are naturally available within any significant artist's canon. But only Elvis (and Beatles) fans have taken the time to isolate and value every one.

RCA in late 1955, RCA turned around and reissued the original Elvis Sun recordings with the RCA label in place. And while those RCA reissues have collector value, it is the Sun originals that are coveted.

That's All Right/Blue Moon of Kentucky (Sun 209, 1954): **$10,000**

Good Rockin' Tonight/I Don't Care If the Sun Don't Shine (Sun 210, 1954): **$3,500**

Milkcow Blues Boogie/You're a Heartbreaker (Sun 215, 1955): **$5,000**

Baby Let's Play House/I'm Left, You're Right, She's Gone (Sun 217, 1955): **$3,000**

I Forgot to Remember to Forget/Mystery Train (Sun 223, 1955): **$2,500**

Elvis with record producer Sam Phillips, Leo Soroka and Robert Johnson at Sun Recording Studio, 1956.
Colin Escott/Michael Ochs Archives/Getty Images

For both the specialist and the general collector, Elvis' career is most easily broken down into four basic categories. His early years with Sun, and the first with RCA devour the bulk of his 1950s output, and it is here that we hear (and see him) at his most incendiary, churning out the hits that remain most people's first thought when considering his work – "Heartbreak Hotel," "Jailhouse Rock," "Love Me Tender," "Baby, Let's Play House" and so forth.

The 1960s were largely devoured by his movie soundtrack recordings, a corpus of 15 albums that it is very easy to mock, but which nevertheless includes some fabulous, and very successful, recordings; and then there is the

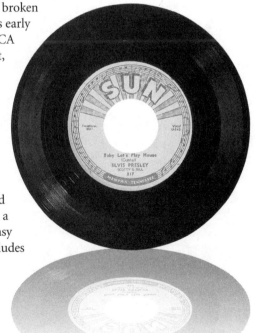

sudden reappearance of Elvis the rootsy rocker, first broadcast on the 1968 NBC TV special, and extending through the last years of the sixties and across such subsequent albums as *From Memphis to Vegas / From Vegas to Memphis* and *Elvis Country*. And finally, there is Elvis the icon, the jumpsuit-and-rhinestones bedecked showman born onstage in Las Vegas and spread across the last years of his life.

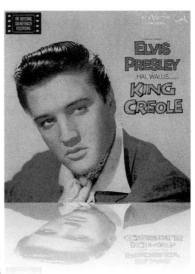

These eras are not inclusive. Among the soundtracks can be found the late fifties showpieces *Loving You* and *King Creole*, both of which are essential to any appreciation of that period; throughout his career, there were the gospel and Christmas albums that did so much to broaden his appeal beyond the rock and pop audience he originally courted.

Live recordings, dating back to his formative days performing at the Louisiana Hayride, offer an entirely different view on Elvis' career—it seems incredible today to consider that his first official live album (the aforementioned *From Memphis to Vegas / From Vegas to Memphis*) did not appear until 1969, but the archives have opened many times since then, to offer us glimpses into any number of shows.

Indeed, we are fortunate that the tapes were rolling at any number of key concerts—the Hayride tapes represent many people's first exposure to Elvis in concert; a recording made aboard the USS Arizona in 1961 marked his last show for seven years (find it on the Elvis Aron Presley box set). 1968 saw him back in action for the benefit of the NBC cameras, and the epochal Elvis TV special; 1969 brought his Las Vegas debut; 1972 saw him headline Madison Square; 1973 brought a worldwide satellite broadcast from Hawaii; and on June 27, 1977, he was recorded live at the Market Square Arena, Indianapolis, at the last concert he would ever play.

All of these, and many more besides, have now been released, some by RCA and its subsequent owners; some through less official channels; and some by Follow That Dream, established in 1999 as the Official Elvis Presley Collectors label, and responsible now for some of the most laudably curated compilations and collections that any artist's catalog can boast. That these are all largely confined to CD-only is a drawback that every vinyl collector must learn to live with. But Elvis collectors in general have never had it so good.

In as much as they were all released as limited editions, many of the Follow That Dream CDs are now very hard to find, and highly-priced too—

some even vie with original vinyl in terms of value. For the true rarities in the Elvis catalog, however, it is vinyl that leads the way, beginning with August 1956's *TV Guide Presents Elvis Presley.*

That month saw Elvis interviewed by journalist Paul Wilder, backstage at the Polk Theatre, Lakeland, Florida, to coincide with a three-part Elvis feature appearing in the magazine. Copies of the interview were pressed and mailed out to select radio stations; four excerpts which include Elvis musing on his Pelvis nickname ("it's one of the most childish expressions I ever heard coming from an adult"), and a brief interview with Colonel Tom Parker, which took place while Elvis was onstage, performing "Heartbreak Hotel."

"We are informed by RCA that this [record] represents the very first occasion on which the famous Presley voice has appeared on record... sans music," one of the two accompanying inserts remarked. "If this constitutes a collectors' item, make the most of it." The latest Goldmine price guide values it at $1,500, and while that is some way short of making it the most valuable Elvis record in the world (as the liner notes to the compilation *A Legendary Performer Volume 3* insisted), it's still a worthy addition to the collection.

The most valuable of all Elvis records is, in fact, his very first recording. In January, 2015, Third Man Records founder Jack White paid $300,000 for the only existing copy of "My Happiness" and "That's When Your Heartaches Begin," a 10-inch acetate recorded by Elvis in July 1953, as a gift for his friend Ed Leek. (It was Leek's daughter who placed the disc on sale.)

Famously, this is the recording that first alerted Sun Records founder Sam Philips to Presley's talent (Philips owned the studio where the acetate was recorded); and, of course, for more than 60 years, it was one that would escape every collector's clutches. Just months after his purchase, however, White reissued the disc for Record Store Day, a limited edition "so close to the historic original as to almost be indistinguishable from one other." Prices for the reissue are themselves steadily rising (copies currently sell for around $125), but at least it is now attainable.

Other major Elvis rarities are equally eye-catching—in India, his singles were issued on 78 until as late as 1966, discs that are highly prized both for their rarity and their anachronistic appeal (the last Elvis 78 issued in the U.S. was "I Got Stung," some six years previous.)

The aforementioned Sun singles are always in demand—in 2015, a set of five in Near-Mint condition sold for $3,250), with their 78 equivalents even more so. And, for the collector who must have everything, there is the *International Hotel, Las Vegas Nevada, Presents Elvis*, 1969 box set, featuring stock copies of a couple of LPs, together with three photos, sundry ephemera and a thank-you note from Elvis and the Colonel. And who could ever pass up on the promotional triple EPs, rounding up Elvis's entire debut album across three 7-inch discs, that came free with the purchase of an RCA Victor

Victrola record player in 1956?

There are other treasures, however, that are considerably less instantly recognizable—copies of 1973's *Aloha from Hawaii via Satellite* bearing a sticker advertising sponsor Van Camp's Chicken of the Sea tuna, for example; or, staying with the same album, it's 7-inch "jukebox album" counterpart. A copy of the "That's All Right"/"Blue Moon Of Kentucky" single on RCA Gold Standard label, with the artist's name misspelled Preseley—one copy sold on ebay for $6,000 in 2011; a copy of the *Speedway* album with the original bonus color photograph still inside is valued at $3,000.

And so many more. Indeed, with more than sixty years worth of recordings and releases to pursue, the fact that so many millions of records were sold is, perhaps, the last consideration that a collector needs to consider. The music is immortal. And its possibilities are infinite.

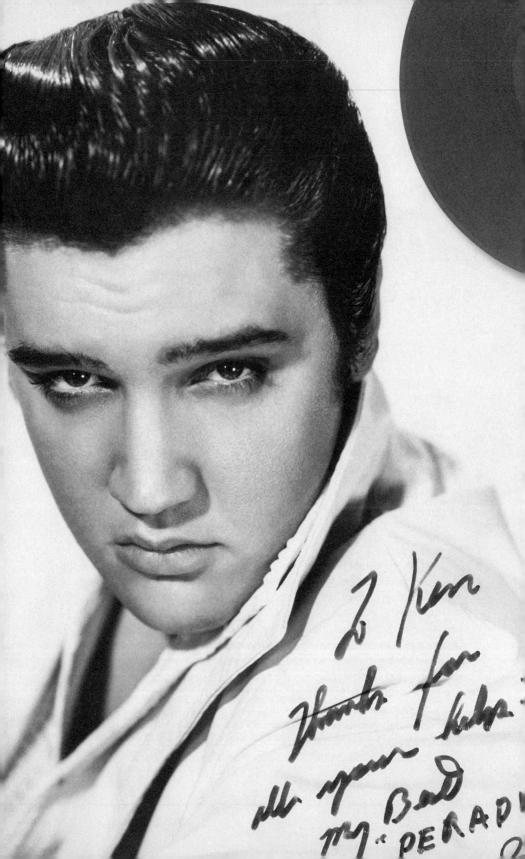

TOP 10 ELVIS RARITIES ON RCA

Elvis Christmas Album (RCA LOC 1035; mono LP red vinyl, 1957): **$20,000**

That's All Right/Blue Moon of Kentucky (RCA Gold Standard 447-0601; red label, misspelled "Preseley"): **$6,000**

Elvis Presley... the Most Talked-About New Personality in the Last Ten Years of Recorded Music (RCA EPB 1254; with picture sleeve, 1956): **$6,000**

Good Luck Charm/ Anything That's Part Of You (RCA 37-7992; 33 rpm 7-inch with picture sleeve, 1962): **$5,000**

Elvis Presley (RCA SPD 23; Triple EP with picture sleeve, 1956): **$5,000**

Aloha from Hawaii (RCA VPSX-6089; promo quadradisc w/Chicken of The Sea sticker on cover, 1973): **$3,500**

This Is His Life: Elvis Presley (Mystery Train/I Forgot To Remember) (RCA 47-6357; promo 45 with picture sleeve, 1955): **$3,000**

Elvis Gold Records Vol. 4 (RCA LPM-3921; mono promo LP, Indianapolis pressing, 1968): **$3,000**

Speedway (RCA LPM 3989; mono promo LP with sticker and color photo, 1968): **$3,000**

His Latest Flame/Little Sister (RCA 37-7908; 33 rpm 7-inch with picture sleeve, 1961): **$3,000**

The Rolling Stones photographed by legendary rock photographer Ian Wright while on tour in 1964 at the Globe Theatre in Stockton on Tees, England. The tour supported the Stones' first hit, "I Wanna be Your Man," a song written by Paul McCartney and John Lennon.
Image courtesy Heritage Auctions

10

MONO: MUSIC FOR THE ONE-TRACK MIND

ALL THE MODERN TALK ABOUT a "vinyl revival" is in many ways deceptive. More new vinyl is being released, that is true, and more is being purchased, too. But the secondary market... used records, old cut-outs, vintage pressings and so forth... has never gone away, or even looked like doing so.

Even at the height of the compact disc's popularity, with the mainstream music business convinced that it had seen the last of LPs and singles, record fairs around the world remained full of vinyl and vinyl collectors.

While market forces bemoaned the proliferation of illegal downloading and insurgent streaming services, and predicted the end of music as we know it, dealers continued merrily setting up their stalls and laying out their wares. And while the industry tried to win back its customers by rolling out ever more stunning new technology (SACD, DVD-A, blu-ray etc), a lot of collectors moved in the opposite direction entirely, to seek out the most primitive sound of all... mono.

Mono is where recorded sound began. A one-track recorder and a single microphone, capturing exactly what was going on in the room at the time of recording. There was no overdubbing, little tape manipulation, nothing that you could "fix in the mix." And when you played it back, whether you had one speaker or a hundred, the sound was the same from each one.

Of course the technology improved over time, first in the studios and then in the home. Early in the 1950s, guitar legend Les Paul was among

the first to experiment with what would become known as "stereo sound"—splitting different elements of the signal between two speakers; and, by the late 1950s, the first recording studios were equipping themselves with the resultant equipment.

It remained a minority pursuit, however. When Elvis Presley cut his first stereo session in 1957, he did so only because the regular mono recording equipment had broken down, and it would be 1960 before he released his first stereo album (*Elvis Is Back!*).

Slowly, however, the new format began to gain in popularity, and by the time the British Invasion reached these shores, most albums were being produced in both mono and stereo—regardless of whether or not they were actually recorded in stereo in the first place.

The marvels of "electronic processing" allowed engineers to create at least a rudimentary stereo effect, usually by splitting the vocals into one channel, and the instrumentation into the other. The results were usually as horrible as that description suggests, but for many people growing up at that time, it's how their old records are supposed to sound.

By the mid-1960s, it was clear that stereo was here to stay, and that mono was destined for the dustbin. Record labels even began preparing their customers for the inevitable, with a note on the back (usually) of every mid-late 1960s mono album you own: "this high fidelity monaural recording is scientifically designed to play with the highest quality of reproduction on the phonograph of your choice, new or old.

"If you are the owner of a new stereophonic system, this record will play with even more brilliant true-to-life fidelity. In short, you can purchase this record with no fear of its becoming obsolete in the future."

And it was true. Lovingly cared for and kept scratch-and-crackle free, a record purchased in 1966 will sound as good as it did 50 years before. And there are precious few modern commodities that you can say that for.

No, mono was made to last and, more than any other sonic delivery system, it has. Even stereo has been knocked down and gnawed at by modern surround sound, while quadraphonic never really got off the blocks in the first place.

Mono's fortunes may have risen and fallen. It may have been declared dead more than once, and spent so long in hiding that Rip Van Winkle feels threatened by it. But collectors never forgot it, and they never tired of searching for it, either.

It isn't simply an affectation, either. No two ears will ever agree whether mono really does *sound* better than stereo, although it can certainly be more powerful. But the very act of recording in mono delivered a sonic statement of intent, as the Rolling Stones 1960s producer, Andrew Loog Oldham, explains.

"We recorded everything in mono. Someone else [mixed it into] stereo when we were away on tour or wherever. They knew we wouldn't have the time to go looking at our records in the stores, so they just went ahead and did it. If you want to hear the Stones as we intended you to hear them, listen to the original mono albums."

Today we can do that (at least for the most part), thanks to the Stones's *In Mono* box set, which preserves all of the band's 1960s albums bar the live *Got Live if You Want It* in living, sparkling monophonic sound.

Prior to the 2016 unveiling of that beast, however, the search for Stones in mono was the same as the search for almost any band. Beset by difficulty.

It was 1968 when manufacturers in the United States (a year or so later in the UK, and the same again in various other countries), decreed that mono releases were a thing of the past.

A few records did still make out in that format for radio promotion— as late as 1973, in fact, Atlantic Records released a tiny quantity of Led Zeppelin's *Houses of the Holy* album in that format; and promotional singles continued to appear in both stereo (on one side) and mono (on the other) for some years more.

So far as the general consumer was concerned, however, no new mono releases were being produced, no older mono albums were being repressed. Indeed, among the modern mono collector's most avid dreams is the wish for a time machine to swirl back to the early 1970s. For, just as countless vinyl collections made their way to the used store in the late 1980s, as compact discs swept into replace them, so countless mono albums took a similar journey, as their owners invested in the few stereo versions.

They gained a second ear full of sounds and effects. But they lost so much more.

It's by no means a hard and fast rule, but many bands treated their mono and stereo releases as very separate sonic statements. The track listing would be the same, and the artwork too. But different mixes, different timings, and sometimes even completely different performances were the hallmarks of what are now the most legendary mono albums, and they proliferate elsewhere, too.

Yes, there are some very valuable mono albums out there to taunt and haunt the collector. But the prime incentive for walking these paths is the utterly different listening experience that will soon be enfolding you whatever you pay, and whatever you buy.

One of my own favorite mono albums is the debut album by Claudine Longet, the succinctly titled *Claudine* (A&M LP 121). I couldn't tell you why, couldn't tell you what is different to the stereo version. It just sounds… better.

Furthermore, many bands—as Oldham has already remarked—cared only for their mono mix, and left the stereo to other hands entirely. To them, all this new-flangled two-speaker nonsense was still a novelty, and one that had nothing to do with their core audience, as George Martin, producer of the Beatles, later elaborated.

"Very few people had stereo equipment. Almost everyone listened on mono; it was accepted as the standard. Stereo was strictly for the hi-fi freaks."

Frequently, too, stereo albums cost up to a buck more than mono, and that made a difference as well. It was only as record prices came down, and the cost of stereo record players followed, that the new format became accepted, but as late as 1967, many bands still viewed stereo with suspicion.

According to Beatle John Lennon, "you haven't heard *Sgt. Pepper* [*'s Lonely Hearts Club Band*] if you haven't heard it in mono," and aficionados will happily document the manifold differences that you will hear when you do so.

Some of them are minor; a dash of guitar at the end of the opening title

"YOU HAVEN'T HEARD SGT. PEPPER ['S LONELY HEARTS CLUB BAND] IF YOU HAVEN'T HEARD IT IN MONO..."
-JOHN LENNON

The Beatles with producer George Martin in Abbey Road Studios, London, January 1967.
Image courtesy Apple Corps Ltd.

track and a few extra drum beats at the beginning of its reprise. But others are instantly noticeable—"She's Leaving Home" is slower, and a lot more effective in mono; "Lucy in the Sky with Diamonds" pumps up the echo around Lennon's vocal; "Fixing a Hole" is longer and the barnyard cacophony that introduces "Good Morning" recruits some radically different sounds.

The Beatles' albums are by far the most intently studied of all mono catalogs, with sundry websites offering almost second-by-second guides to every single variation on display. But there are many, many more albums out there that will repay a careful listen or two, and some that don't even need that. The differences will leap out and tear your head off.

For instance....

The Beatles: *The Beatles* (the "White" album) (UK Apple PMC 7068)

There is more farmyard foolishness to be found in the mono "Piggies," a different barrage of screaming in "Everybody's Got Something To Hide (Except Me and My Monkey)"; and a longer guitar break during "Honey

Pie." But the most noticeable shift is in the extraordinarily fiery presentation of "Helter Skelter" that might trim almost 50 seconds from the stereo version, but amply compensates in terms of aggression.

The Jeff Beck Group: *Truth* (UK Columbia SX 6293)

The instrumental "Beck's Bolero" features an excellent extended conclusion which was deleted from the stereo pressing.

The Crazy World of Arthur Brown: *Crazy World of Arthur Brown* (UK Track 612 005)

U.S. editions of the first four Beatles albums aside, this was the first mono mix *to ma*ke it onto CD alongside its stereo counterpart—at least partially. Side one alone was selected for release, and deservedly so. The opening three cuts ("Prelude," "Nightmare" and the hit "Fire") are each longer in mono, while "Fire" itself loses the trumpets that hallmarked the stereo, and sounds far more menacing as a consequence. Even more noticeably, however, the remainder of the side is a completely different performance, and boasts a completely different construction, too.

Side two, on the other hand, is somewhat less remarkable.

Richard and Mimi Fariña: *Reflections in a Crystal Mind* (Vanguard 79204)

The mono mix is a lot less flowery and cluttered than the stereo; a lot more aggressive too (for example, John Hammond's harmonica far more to the fore during "Hard Loving Loser"). The stereo deliberately brought more instrumentation to the fore, presumably to give headphone listeners a treat. In mono, this remarkable LP feels more like a wall of sound.

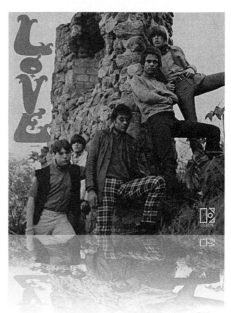

Trini Lopez: *Live at PJs* (Reprise R6093)

Most notable for a completely different live version of "La Bamba"!

Love: *Love* (Elektra EKL 4001)

A few slightly longer (15 to 20 seconds) tracks, and a far more pounding mix give the mono album a very different feel to the stereo.

Pink Floyd: *Piper at the Gates of Dawn* (Tower T 5903)

While mono remained the norm for older acts like The Beatles and the Stones, the new wave of psychedelic bands were automatically drawn to stereo, where the sonic possibilities felt endless. Floyd, Hendrix, Jefferson Airplane, all crammed their records with the weirdest effects they could, panning guitars from speaker to speaker, separating the drums, conjuring eerie echoes and so forth.

Played back in mono, very different soundscapes are conjured, although the keen ear will also discern less subjective differences. Here, "Interstellar Overdrive" is presented in a different mix; "Flaming" packs a different intro and "Pow R Toc H," packs more vocal effects.

The Velvet Underground: *White Light White Heat* (Verve V 5046)

If you know this album in stereo, you are already familiar with its behemothic weight. Amplify that for the mono mix, but remember, too—the stereo album provides a hidden bonus track in the form of "The Gift"; switch off the channel that relays the vocal, and you can hear the band playing the instrumental "Booker T" in the other. In mono!

The Who: *The Who Sell Out* (Decca DL 4950)

Preparing the CD reissue of this classic album, producer Jon Astley explained, "I did digital copies [of the mono and stereo versions], compared them... and it sounds better in mono."

Sounds better, *is* better. The mono version of "Our Love Was" is substantially different, boasting an entirely different guitar solo. There is less cross-fading between the songs and the "advertisements" that punctuate them, and though some ears accuse the mono mix of a certain clumsiness, to others it adds to the album's authenticity—the original concept was a tribute to Britain's recently outlawed pirate radio stations, blasting mono pop music across the country from ships moored outside the country's territorial waters. And the mono mix sounds just like they did.

The above list is dominated, for perhaps obvious reasons, by albums hailing from the late 1960s, by which time stereo was already established, and new mono releases were difficult to find even at the time—today, mono copies of Simon & Garfunkel's Bookends album are valued at anything up to $800 (NM, with the enclosed poster) not for any sonic variations, but simply because it's so hard to find.

Track back a few years, however, and an astonishing collection can be gleaned from the British Invasion that The Beatles heralded. Go back even further, and there are some spectacular mono classical recordings just begging for rediscovery.

The familiarity of so much of the material lends itself easily to straightforward mono-stereo comparisons; and again, we must remember that the bands themselves were rarely involved in the stereo mix. That was left to engineers whose own brief included making sure that the stereo offered listeners something to make them go "wow."

Instruments and incidents rendered inaudible by the stereo process club the unsuspecting listener over the head. Returning to The Beatles, the intro to "From Me To You" features a harmonica overdub in mono completely absent from the stereo version, while "And I Love Her" even varies between mono versions. That issued on the American United Artists soundtrack has a single-track vocal (with harmonies); on British Parlophone pressings, however, they are almost completely double-tracked.

They are little differences to be sure, but they're significant ones, and the pursuit of further examples certainly makes an interesting pursuit. Following on from the Stones mono box, a similar gathering of the Kinks's 1960s mono hit the streets, but whether you listen to them or to their 50-year-old originals, anybody who grew up on the mock-stereo versions of the first few LPs will be blown away.

Indeed, it is true that often the joys of mono are best appreciated only when you come to them after years of exposure to a particularly clumsy stereo mix. Freddie & the Dreamers' eponymous debut, for instance, was stereo-fied with even more horrific separation than The Beatles albums endured.

It is not the worst offender, however.

The Hollies' "Bus Stop" ranks amongst the most exquisite songs, not to mention performances, in that band's entire canon. But it was not until 1993's *30th Anniversary Collection* CD that an even remotely acceptable stereo mix became available.

Prior to that, if you wanted to hear "Bus Stop" without your eardrums blistering in protest, you needed to seek out the mono mix. The essential

The Rolling Stones

idea of stereo is that the listener should get an audio picture of where every instrument (or voice) was situated during the original recording. According to the stereo *Hollies Greatest Hits* album, "Bus Stop" was taped with the band's vocal chorus standing at one.

Another example of mono better capturing the spirit of a recording session can be grasped from the Rolling Stones' 1966 "Have You Seen Your Mother, Baby (Standing In The Shadows)." According to Andrew Oldham, the song's distinctive introduction was recorded, late in the day at a Hollywood Sound session, by Mick Jagger, Keith Richards and Oldham himself, standing around a microphone pinching their noses and singing "na na na." (Or words to that effect.) The sound complimented an otherwise weak guitar figure.

Studio trickery disguises the sound's origins in both stereo and mono, but on the latter, at least, it gave the song an other-worldly psychedelic feel which even the following year's *Their Satanic Majesties Request* (the last U.S. Stones album to be released in mono) would be unable to recapture. And when "Have You Seen Your Mother, Baby" turned up on the radio, it had an immediacy which left the year's other innovators at the starting post.

Because mono was made for radio play, and even in these days of digital perfection, reissued classics seldom sound exactly like you remember them; neither will they, until you dig out that scratchy old original, and crank it up really high. And if "Don't Let The Sun Catch You Crying" suddenly sounds that fresh again, how will the rest of Gerry and the Pacemakers' first album sound in mono?

Excellent, of course! And commercial considerations notwithstanding, that is why so many labels have seen fit to return to those old tapes and give them another airing, both on CD and on vinyl—beginning as far back as 1980, when Capitol Records reissued a handful of vintage albums (the Hollies' *Greatest Hits* included) in mono.

Most of the era's heaviest hitters have now seen their canons recounted in mono, with Bob Dylan's mono catalog a startling upgrade on its

ROCK IN MONO –
25 TOP RARITIES

Rolling Stones: *12 x 5* (London (maroon label with unboxed logo) LL3402, 1964) current value: **$10,000**

Rolling Stones: *Big Hits* (High Tide and Green Grass) (With two lines of type on the front cover, all in small letters) (London NP1, 1966) current value: **$8,000**

Ike & Tina Turner: *River Deep -- Mountain High* (Philles PHLP4011,1967) current value: **$8,000**

Jimi Hendrix: *Electric Ladyland* (Reprise 2R6307, 1968) current value: **$6,000**

The Beatles: *...and Frank Ifield on Stage* (Vee Jay LP1085,1964) current value: **$6,000**

Jimi Hendrix Experience: *Axis: Bold As Love* (Reprise R6281,1968) current value: **$5,000**

Bob Dylan: *Blonde on Blonde* (Columbia C2L41,1966) current value: **$4,000**

Elvis Presley: *Speedway* (RCA Victor LPM-3989,1968) current value: **$3,500**

Led Zeppelin: *Houses of the Holy* (Atlantic 7255,1973) current value: **$3,000**

Rolling Stones: *Sticky Fingers* (Rolling Stones COC59100,1971) current value: **$2,500**

Led Zeppelin: *Led Zeppelin* (Atlantic 8216,1969) current value: **$2,000**

Led Zeppelin: *II* (Atlantic 8236,1969) current value: **$2,000**

Elvis Presley: *Gold Records, Volume 4* (RCA Victor LPM-3921,1968) current value: **$2,000**

The Velvet Underground: *White Light/White Heat* (Verve V-5046,1967) current value: **$2,000**

The Velvet Underground: *...and Nico* (Verve V-5008,1967) current value: **$2,000**

The Beatles: *Ain't She Sweet* (Atco 33-169,1964) current value: **$1,500**

Led Zeppelin: *III* (Atlantic 7201,1970) current value: **$1,500**

stereo counterpart. But lesser-feted acts, too, have reappeared on vinyl—recent years have seen reissues for such unsung heroes of 1960s psych as the Gods, Tomorrow, Rainbow Ffolly and July, alongside the expected Doors, Jefferson Airplane and Grateful Dead.

Neither does the fun end with the traditional death of mono. In 1974 the British R&B band Dr Feelgood caused considerable stir when they insisted on releasing their debut album, *Down by the Jetty*, in mono only. So much so, in fact, that their U.S. label refused to release it.

Two years later, the Ramones' label *did* agree to that band's debut being issued in mono; this time, it was the distributors who baulked, meaning the dream was left on the shelf for the next 40 years.

In 2016, however, original producer Craig Leon returned to the tapes

The Crickets: *The "Chirping" Crickets* (Brunswick BL54038,1958) current value: **$1,500**

Gene Vincent: *...Rocks! And the Blue Caps Roll* (Capitol T970,1958) current value: **$1,500**

Buddy Holly: *That'll Be the Day* (Decca DL8707,1958) current value: **$1,500**

The Doors: *Waiting for the Sun* (Elektra EKL-4024,1968) current value: **$1,500**

Bob Dylan: *Highway 61 Revisited* (Columbia CL2389,1965) current value: **$1,000**

Elvis Presley: *Elvis* (RCA Victor LPM-1382,,1956) current value: **$1,000**

The Beatles: *...Vs The Four Seasons* (Vee Jay DX-30,1964) current value: **$1,000**

The Mothers of Invention: *We're Only in It for the Money* (Verve V-5045,1968) current value: **$1,000**

Gabba Gabba Hey! It's the Ramones in 1976 at The Roundhouse in London.
Gus Stewart/Getty Images

and gave *The Ramones* the treatment it was intended to have, with added count-ins, added weight, and a monstrous roar that reminds you of the very first time you heard it, on whatever passed for your stereo system back in 1976. Without the stereo intrusions, of course.

Of course purists will tell you that you're still not buying the "real thing"; that the album as the artist originally presented it, recorded, mixed and pressed on the technology of the day, is a very different creature to the modern recreation, made with machinery the original studio team could never have dreamed might exist.

But, in mono and every other field too, some records are so rare, so expensive, or simply so impossible to find in tip-top condition that that argument is rendered redundant.

You can only collect the things you can find. Everything else goes onto the wants list.

DYLAN, BAEZ AND THE FOLK ROCK BOOM

ANYTHING CAN CHANGE A PERSON'S, or a generation's, collecting habits.

The emergence of such eighties super groups as Foreigner and Asia sent many fans searching back through the individual members' back catalogs—and acquiring a love for British progressive rock that still blazes bright throughout the hobby today.

When Nirvana broke through in the early nineties, punk rock returned to prominence and, again, has not faltered since then.

More recently, the publication of Amanda Petrusich's *Do Not Sell At Any Price*, and a succession of magnificently curated CD collections by such labels as Old Hat, Dust to Digital and Third Man, have awakened a fresh curiosity for the world of 78s.

David Hajdu's book *Positively 4th Street: The Lives and Times of Joan Baez, Bob Dylan, Mimi Baez Fariña & Richard Fariña* was another such moment. Dylan has always been a popular topic among collectors, his vast discography littered with vibrant rarities and hidden treasures.

Baez and the Fariñas, on the other hand, were scarcely acknowledged, and moving beyond their careers and into all the others that their lives touched, allowed collectors to open the door to an entire new world of music.

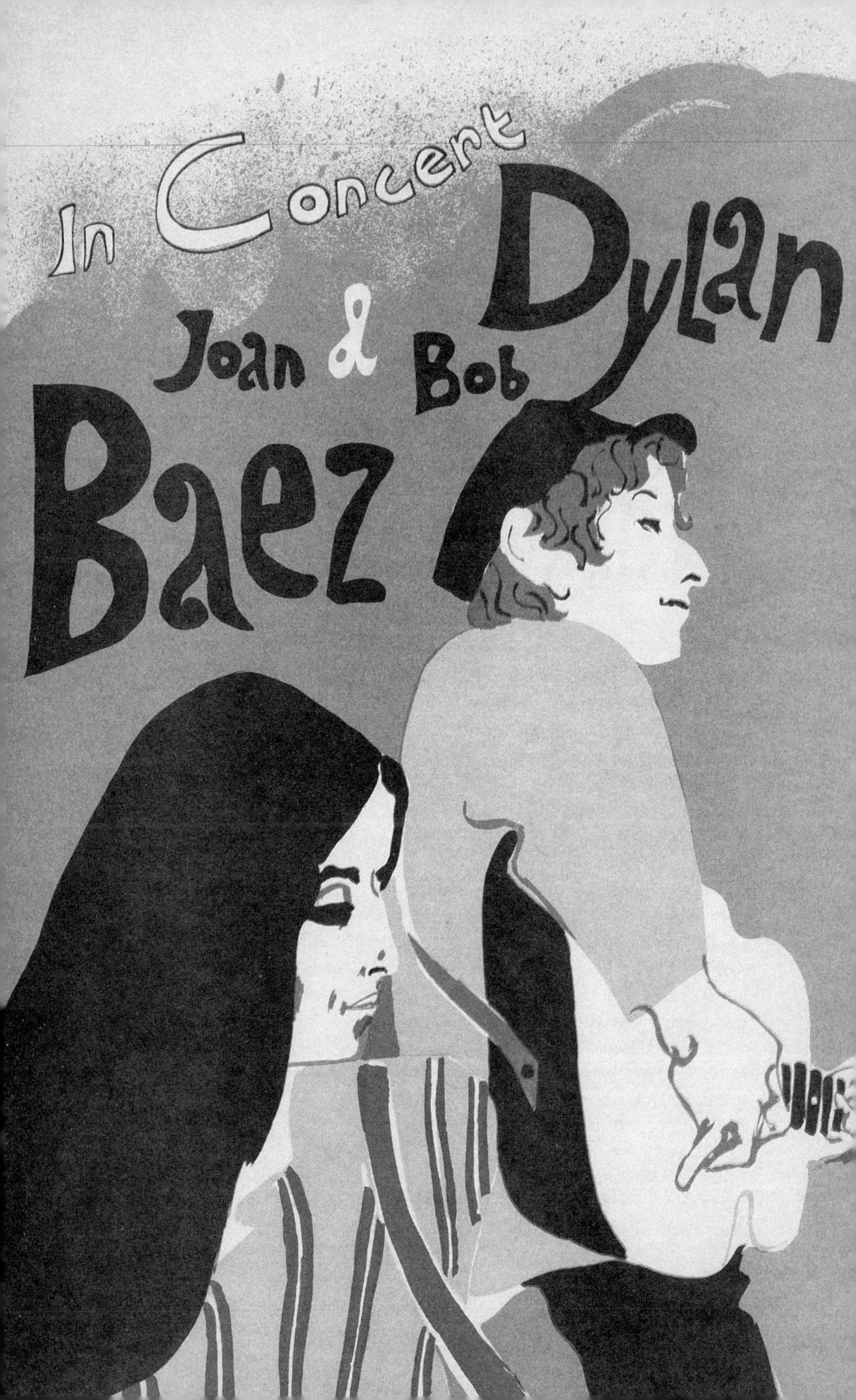
In Concert
Joan & Bob
Baez Dylan

To many of them, after all, the Folk boom of the early 1960s was little more than the Top Forty hits of Peter, Paul and Mary; the moms-and-dads appeal of the Weavers; and never-ending choruses of "Michael, Row the Boat Ashore."

Now, however, such names as Eric Von Schmidt, Caroline Hester, Rambling Jack Elliot and the Fariñas themselves came to prominence, *not* as adjuncts to the Dylan discography, as they had hitherto been regarded, but as essential artists in their own right.

newport folk festival
july 22-25 1965

Dylan shook the Folk Music world when he debuted an electric guitar set at the 1965 Newport Jazz Festival.
Image courtesy Heritage Auctions

The reputation of the annual Newport Festival shifted overnight from being the old-fashioned, comfortable institution that Dylan shook up when he "went electric," to a rich, varied, and most of all, far-sighted event that totally predicted the "world music" events of later generations.

The early years of the Elektra label were resurrected, adding founder Jac Holzman's championing of traditional music through the 1950s and early 1960s to the company's later fame as the home of the Doors, Love and the Incredible String Band; and one of the strongholds of west coast singer-songwriters.

The radical politics of the era were re-examined, to establish the music once again as an outsider looking in on the authoritarian attitudes of the Cold War era. And the artistry of the age has blossomed ever since.

◀ A rare 1965 Bob Dylan and Joan Baez concert handbill.
Image courtesy Heritage Auctions

It would be unfair to say that this single book was wholly responsible for the movement's emergence into the collecting field; very likely, it would have happened anyway—again, the restless curiosity of Dylan's fans had already sent values for certain records soaring, while other media, too, focused in on the age.

From the same stable of talent as *This Is Spinal Tap*, the 2003 movie *A Mighty Wind* sought to do to folk what the earlier movie did for heavy metal; and a decade later, the Coen Brothers' *Inside Llewyn Davis* detailed a week in the life of a struggling Greenwich Village folkie on the very eve of Bob Dylan's arrival in the city. They too fed (and still feed) their audience's need to find out more, a fascination that is best met through seeking out the records that blazed the folk trail in the first place.

Nevertheless, Kevin Welk, who, as head of the Vanguard record label, was also custodian of both the Fariñas and a great part of Baez's back catalog, recalled that just a few years before Hajdu's book's publication, his label's catalog was basically moribund, not only untouched but large unsought after.

Only slowly was the company encouraged to begin seriously revisiting its archives in search of forgotten treasures; only gradually did the old tapes receive the benefits of modern remastering. Then *Positively Fourth* Street hit and suddenly Welk was unyielding in his quest to restore the entire label heritage to the racks, knowing full well that even if a particular album or artist has no apparent market relevance today, who knows when a new trend or interest will suddenly raise it to untold heights of popularity?

Positively Fourth Street was one example of that; another dates back to the mid-1990s, and the realization that an entire generation of electronic musicians was taking its lead (and a lot of samples, too) from a pair of LPs which had lain undisturbed in the Vanguard vault since for almost thirty years, the electronic soundscapes of Jean-Jacques Perrey and Gershon Kingsley, *The In Sound From Way Out* and *Kaleidoscopic Vibrations: Spotlight On The Moog.*

Forgotten for so long, these albums were the archetypal bargain bin regulars, and that is where 1990s electro artists, seeking new and unusual samples, rediscovered them. Vanguard pounced and, having commissioned fresh remixes from the likes of Fat Boy Slim and Eurotrash, the label wound up with a 3CD box set of an act that the vast majority of record buyers have never even heard of—let alone purchased at the time. All these years on, it's still a hot seller.

It is (re-)discoveries like that which have established Vanguard among the, indeed, vanguard of collectable American labels, with the company's 1960s output in particular harboring some extravagantly wonderful gems.

Of course, great
swathes of the catalog are a
part of the American furniture
today—Joan Baez, Country Joe
McDonald, Buffy St Marie and the
Weavers require no introduction whatsoever.
Neither does the Newport Folk Festival, with which
Vanguard was inextricably linked from its inception in 1959.

But Vanguard itself never allowed blatant commercial considerations to shape its destiny; nor the casual barriers laid down by generic pigeonholing.

Folk, of course, is one of the oldest forms of music in the world, emerging from what we now regard as "traditional" music—the vast corpus of ballads accumulated in the late 19th century by Harvard professor Francis Child, and which still bear his name today ("the Child Ballads"), sea shanties, cowboy songs, and so forth.

But the field bleeds into so many others. Many of the performers at the first Newport Festivals were bluesmen, lining up alongside bluegrass musicians and hillbilly songsters to prove that "folk" should never be considered the province of the oldest balladeers alone.

That understanding was paramount to Vanguard's success. From the outset, the label's motto insisted, "music for connoisseurs" and so it proved.

Vanguard had never even sniffed a gold record until Joan Baez burst onto the scene, and she remains the company's biggest selling artist. But there are close to 300 other albums released by Vanguard between 1960-69 which repay investigation just as graciously, most of which never came within spitting distance of the chart.

The Vanguard label was launched in June 1950, by the brothers Maynard and Seymour Solomon, built upon a $10,000 advance from their father, Benjamin. The brothers' forte was jazz and classical music and two labels were established to cater for their tastes—Vanguard itself, and The Bach Guild, an ambitious project intended to release recordings of all of its classical composer namesake's chorale work.

Original Vanguard releases, in keeping with industry standards, were issued on 10-inch LPs. Between 1953-55, Vanguard released some 20 different jazz albums in this format, including well-received and respected titles by Vic Dickenson, Sir Charles Thompson, Joe Newman, Buck Clayton, Don Elliott and Ruby Braff—many produced by the legendary John Hammond.

However, a glimmer of the label's future came in the form of Brother John Sellers' *Sings Blues & Folk Songs* collection in 1954 and, in 1956, Vanguard released its first album by Pete Seeger and the Weavers—a courageous move at a time when the group's political stance saw them all-but boycotted by the rest of the industry. (Paul Robeson, another blacklisted performer, joined the Weavers at the label.)

Releases by Martha Schlamme and Cisco Houston followed and, by the end of the 1950s, Vanguard was essentially the biggest folk game in town. It became even bigger following the arrival of Baez, with her immediate pre-eminence immediately prompting Columbia (who actually rejected Baez) to sign their own female folk singer, Carolyn Hester.

That Hester's first husband, Richard Fariña, would later marry Baez's sister, Mimi (while Dylan, who guested on Hester›s first Columbia album, soon became Baez›s consort), is indicative of just how compact the folk scene was at that time; that the Fariñas would then join Baez at Vanguard, on the other hand, proves the wisdom of the Solomons. What nobody could have imagined at the time was how time would bear out so many of their other signings, and other enterprises too.

Vanguard was more than a label, after all. It was also the official chronicler of the Newport Folk Festival, maintaining a stream of albums that served up highlights not only of the headline acts, but also the myriad unknowns who also took the stage.

The Folk Festival developed out of jazz impresario George Wein's Newport (Rhode Island) Jazz Festival, inaugurated in 1954. With tobacconist Louis Lorillard and entrepreneur Albert Grossman also on the team, Wein launched the new event in 1959, with a weekend (July 11/12) long succession of performances and workshops at Freebody Park. It was a successful event, conjuring some smart performances from the likes of Pete Seeger, Pat Clancy, Odetta, Earl Scruggs and Martha Schlamme, as proven by the three volumes of live recordings released later in the year by Vanguard.

History, however, insists that the highlight of the weekend was the unscheduled arrival on the stage—and, from there, the folk scene itself—of the young Joan Baez, a denizen of the Boston coffee house circuit, but a complete unknown in the wider world.

A special guest of singer Bob Gibson, Baez's performance comprised just two duets, "Virgin Mary Had One Son" and "Jordan River." But she stole the show... and the festival itself... and returned the following year as a headliner in her own right. Even her entrance to the festival grounds was an event; she was chauffeured in a Cadillac hearse, with her name emblazoned on the sides in silver tape.

Despite this success (captured across two accompanying LPs on Vanguard, and a third courtesy of Elektra), not until 1963 would the Folk Festival return to the calendar. By which time, the "folk boom" was fully underway.

Spread now over three days, July 26-28, the event was overseen by a non-profit group of folkies—Pete Seeger, Pete Yarrow, Theodore Bikel, Jean Ritchie and Vanguard's own Erik Darling among them. Seventy-plus performers attracted around 47,000 ticket holders, and the six live albums drawn from the event highlight the massive versatility of the "folk" genre, with four volumes devoted to blues, country and bluegrass, old time music and topical songs; and two more wrapping up the event's main attractions—Baez, of course, the Freedom Singers, Jack Elliott, Dave van Ronk, Judy Collins, and a couple of brand new talents, Canadians Ian Tyson and Sylvia Fricker, and Minnesota's Bob Dylan.

The following year, the festival spun off a further five LPs, including two volumes devoted to all the various forms that were now bagged together as "traditional music," and three from the evening concerts, while the event itself proved the resilience of the genre.

The Beatles had arrived, and the British were invading. As writer Stacey

Williams pointed out at the time, sundry "self-appointed Cassandras [were] predicting the demise of the folk music movement, lamenting the plethora of indiscriminate 'hootenannies' and the British-made rock 'n' roll invasion."

Yet here was Newport, as vibrant as ever, and it was only going to get bigger.

The multifarious talents of Buffy Sainte Marie, Tom Paxton, Judy Roderick and Phil Ochs all debuted at the 1964 show, alongside the expected household names, and though a few of the ensuing performances could be considered eccentric by contemporary folk standards, by Vanguard's standards, eccentricity was the spice of life.

Few of the label's signings ever opted for convention and normalcy; indeed, to describe Vanguard as a folk-oriented concern is to utterly belittle the sheer adventurousness that was the Solomons' true nature.

Georgia-born singer-songwriter Patrick Sky, for example, was a dynamically contrary performer; indeed, if there is such a thing as the archetypal Vanguard artist, Sky might well be it. He confounded even his peers; his gentle, reflective songs were, singer Dave Van Ronk memorably mused, "peopled by bits of verse, horrible puns, unprintable lyrics, japes, jibes and a beer river flowing gently over your grandmother's paisley shawl."

But while today, such a description conjures up visions of a Marilyn Manson-esque monster filling our children's ears with oaths and obscenities, *Patrick Sky*, this earlier fiend's 1965 Vanguard LP, turns out to be nothing like that. Or maybe it is. You never heard "damn" on the radio back then, but Sky lets one slip (during the otherwise plaintive "Many A Mile") without even a guilty pause.

The proving ground for many of Vanguard's most adventurous (and far-sighted) signings was the *New Folks* series of various artists collections. Phil Ochs, Lisa Kindred, Bob Jones and Eric Andersen all made their debut via these albums, with the latter rapidly emerging among the label's most reliable performers as the early folk boom settled into its mid-late 1960s reflective rock mode.

His influence was profound. According to legend, it was Andersen's "Come To My Bedside," a cut from 1965's *Today is The Highway*, which persuaded Kris Kristofferson to start writing sultry love songs; and "Violets Of Dawn" (from 1966's *'Bout Changes And Things*), which prompted Leonard Cohen to begin writing songs in the first place.

In fact, *'Bout Changes...* was a significant album all around, as Andersen escaped the Dylan-shaped shadows which haunted his debut, and carved himself—and his entire genre—a new niche altogether. Five years on, Andersen's thoughtful lyricism, stylistic versatility and gifted story-telling would effortlessly explode into the sensitive singer-songwriter boom of the early 1970s—the earnest young men and women whom history now politely

THE NEWPORT FOLK FESTIVAL

ON VINYL, 1959-1965

**Folk Festival At Newport
Volume 1** (Vanguard VRS 2053,
1959) current value: **$30**

Folk Festival At Newport Vol. 2
(Vanguard VRS 2054, 1959) current
value: **$30**

Folk Festival At Newport Vol. 3
(Vanguard VRS 2055, 1959)
current value: **$30**

**The Newport Folk Festival
1960** (Elektra EKL 189)
current value: **$15**

**The Newport Folk Festival
1960 Vol. 1** (Vanguard VRS 9083,
1960) current value: **$30**

**The Newport Folk Festival
1960 Vol. 2** (Vanguard VRS 9084,
1960) current value: **$30**

**The Folk Music Of The
Newport Folk Festival 1959-
1960 Vol. 1** (Folkways Records
FA 2431, 1961) current value: **$60**

**The Folk Music Of The
Newport Folk Festival 1959-
1960 Vol. 2** (Folkways Records
FA 2432, 1961) current value: **$60**

Folk Song and Minstrelsy (4 LP
box set—sides 7/8 only. Classics
Record Library SRL 7624, 1962)
current value: **$25**

THE NEWPORT FOLK FESTIVAL ON VINYL

1959-1965 (CONTINUED)

Newport Broadside (1963 festival)
(Vanguard VRS 9144, 1964)
current value: **$60**

Blues At Newport (Recorded Live
At The Newport Folk Festival 1963)
(Vanguard VRS 9145, 1964)
current value: **$30**

Old Time Music At Newport
(Recorded Live At The Newport Folk
Festival 1963) (Vanguard VRS 9147,
1964) current value: **$20**

**The Newport Folk Festival 1963—
The Evening Concerts: Vol. 1**
(Vanguard VRS 9148, 1964)
current value: **$50**

**The Newport Folk Festival 1963—
The Evening Concerts: Vol. 2**
(Vanguard VRS 9149, 1964)
current value: **$50**

**Traditional Music At Newport
1964 Part 1** (Vanguard VRS 9182,
1965) current value: **$20**

**Traditional Music At Newport
1964 Part 2** (Vanguard VRS 9183,
1965) current value: **$20**

**The Newport Folk Festival 1964
Evening Concerts: Vol. 1**
(Vanguard VRS 9184, 1965)
current value: **$30**

**The Newport Folk Festival
1964—Evening Concerts Vol. 2**
(Vanguard VRS 9185, 1964)
current value: **$30**

**The Newport Folk Festival
1964—Evening Concerts Vol. 3**
(Vanguard VRS 9186, 1964)
current value: **$30**

**American Folk Singers and
Balladeers** (sides 5/6 within
box set, Vanguard SRL-5644, 1964)
current value: **$25**

**Festival—the Newport Folk
Festival 1965** (Vanguard VRS 9225,
1965) current value: **$40**

Legendary Folk Songs (sides 7-10
within box set, Longines Symphonette
Society—no cat) current value: **$20**

**Highlights of the Newport Folk
Festivals** (within the 2 LP set
Greatest Folksingers of the Sixties,
Vanguard VSD 17/18, 1972)
current value: **$15**

recalls as "modern troubadours."

Whether he was aware or not of what he had created, Andersen himself refused to sit still on his blueprint. 'Bout Changes... was still weaving its spell when its maker restlessly turned his back on all it portended, and rerecorded the entire album with a rock band!

The liner notes to 'Bout Changes And Things Take Two complete the tale, and offer another vivid illustration of Vanguard's modus operandi of the time. As Andersen explained, "We asked Maynard Solomon... and he saw no reason why we couldn't make a new album with the songs from the last one. It hadn't been done before, but what did that matter?"

It didn't matter at all. It's impossible to play favorites between the two albums (although many people try); impossible to say which direction Andersen should have pursued next.

Not that it would have mattered, as he promptly swung off on yet another different course. Andersen's next album, 1968's frustratingly lightweight More Hits From Tin Can Alley, was his last in either a folk or rock mode; the following year, he relocated to Nashville, seeing out his Vanguard contract with the aptly titled A Country Dream.

Which just goes to reinforce one fact. Vanguard was never simply a folk label, and its artists were never simply folkies.

Remarkable new talents continued to flow from the old wellspring, however. Jonathan and Leigh were a somewhat consumptive looking duo who hid in big black overcoats, but cut one lovely album of acoustic musings, Third And Main, for the label in 1967.

In a similar vein, Steve Gillette's eponymous album that same year has a bold other-worldliness that defies simple categorization—and is, in any case, the only LP ever to feature Buffy Sainte-Marie playing coat hangers.

The key, however, is not that these artists were great singers. They were also great songwriters, and it was their efforts (among others, of course) showed that Dylan was not alone in proving that "folk singers" did not have to sing "folk music"—at least in its most traditional form.

That was not news to the cognoscenti, of course. After all, Woody Guthrie and Pete Seeger, perhaps the two most important pre-Dylan influences upon what we now call folk music, were both songwriters in their own right, with Guthrie at least seemingly undergoing a fresh rediscovery by every generation.

Let us also not forget that Ewan MacColl, one of the giants of British traditional music, also wrote "The First Time Ever I Saw Your Face," one of the best-loved soul ballads of all time.

For the collector first entering these waters, perhaps the easiest point of entry will be the dollar bins. There, overlooked releases on the academically inclined Caedmon and Folkways labels can still be found rubbing jackets with the unwanted detritus of pop and rock; folk compilations that were released at budget prices back then can still be found for budget prices today; and so forth.

Buy them, play them, learn from them. And then move on into the later work of the original artists, or onto the fresh pastures that the Folk Boom unleashed—the aforementioned singer-songwriters of the American early 70s (Joni Mitchell, James Taylor and so forth, so many of whom came out of the folk clubs); or the folk rockers of the UK—Fairport Convention, Steeleye Span, Pentangle and the Incredible String Band. The possibilities are both endless and eternal.

As in every other field of collecting, it would be the easiest thing in the world to simply follow the crowd and pledge your wallet to amassing a great Bob Dylan collection. But how much more rewarding to allow your own ears to guide you, with just a favorite instrument, or favorite label, to act as a signpost?

20 FOLK CLASSICS

Buffy Sainte Marie: *It's My Way* (Vanguard VSD 79142, 1964) 2016 value: **current value: $60**

Carolyn Hester: *Carolyn Hester* (Columbia CL 1796, 1962— features Bob Dylan) current value: **$100**

The Cumberland Three: *Folk Scene U.S.A.* (Roulette SR25121, 1960) current value: **$30**

Dave Van Ronk: *Sings Earthy Ballads and Blues* (Folkways FA-2383, 1961) current value: **$50**

Dick [Richard] Fariña & Eric Von Schmidt: *Dick Fariña & Eric Von Schmidt* (Folklore F-LEUT/7, 1963) current value: **$175**

Ewan MacColl: *Scots Street Songs* (Riverside RLP 12612, 1956) current value: **$100**

Harry Belafonte: *The Midnight Special* (RCA Victor LPM 2449, 1962—features Bob Dylan) current value: **$40**

Joan Baez: *Joan Baez* (Vanguard VSD-2077, 1960) current value: **$50**

As for Bob Dylan himself....

Across a career that has now spanned more than half a century; which in turn has established him as the longest-running continually active American artist of the vinyl age (Cliff Richard, recording since 1958, tops the UK listing), Dylan's career as a collectible artist deserves an entire volume to itself; and, of course, it has received many.

His discography devours over 300 listings across the course of the *Goldmine* price guides—considerably fewer than Elvis, with over 1,800; The Beatles, with close to 1,300; and the Stones and the Beach Boys, both of whom are closing in on 500.

Yet that discography includes some of the most sought-after records in the guides; and some of the most avidly collected, too. A full collection of his original mono albums; or a stereo set that aims for original pressings, are both reasonable ambitions to pursue, but neither is as easy as it sounds.

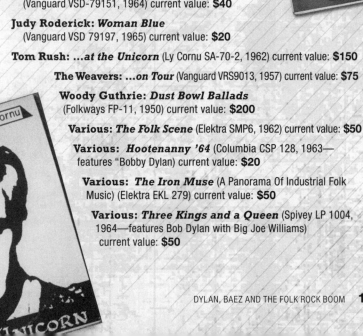

The Kingston Trio: *The Kingston Trio*
(Capitol T996, 1958) current value: **$50**

Pete Seeger: *A Pete Seeger Sampler*
(Folkways FA-2043, 1954) current value: **$150**

Phil Ochs: *In Concert* (Elektra EKL-310, 1966)
current value: **$25**

Ramblin' Jack Elliott: *Jack Elliott*
(Vanguard VSD-79151, 1964) current value: **$40**

Judy Roderick: *Woman Blue*
(Vanguard VSD 79197, 1965) current value: **$20**

Tom Rush: *...at the Unicorn* (Ly Cornu SA-70-2, 1962) current value: **$150**

The Weavers: *...on Tour* (Vanguard VRS9013, 1957) current value: **$75**

Woody Guthrie: *Dust Bowl Ballads*
(Folkways FP-11, 1950) current value: **$200**

Various: *The Folk Scene* (Elektra SMP6, 1962) current value: **$50**

Various: *Hootenanny '64* (Columbia CSP 128, 1963—
features "Bobby Dylan) current value: **$20**

Various: *The Iron Muse* (A Panorama Of Industrial Folk
Music) (Elektra EKL 279) current value: **$50**

Various: *Three Kings and a Queen* (Spivey LP 1004,
1964—features Bob Dylan with Big Joe Williams)
current value: **$50**

Joan Baez and Bob Dylan performing Aug. 28, 1963, at the March On Washington.
Rowland Scherman/National Archives/Getty Images

No less than The Beatles (or a lot of other artists, for that matter), Dylan's discography is a minefield of variations—his 1962 debut album, for example exists in eight different versions issued within just four years!

These include mono and stereo, of course, but also the promotional pressing, with the beloved six "eye" logos on label and "A New Star on Columbia" sticker on cover; another six "eye" label but printed in black and red as opposed to the traditional orange; a "Guaranteed High Fidelity" variation; and the "360 Sound Stereo" label, with the new legend in either black or white.

Needless to say, all vary greatly in value, but a common joke among Dylan collectors is that that is nothing new. Simply maintaining a complete collection of Dylan's regular releases can become both incredibly cash- and space-consuming, as anybody following the on-going *Bootleg Series* of rarities and unreleased material will know.

After a succession of two or three disc packages, volume ten contained four CDs; volume eleven carried six; volume 12 held 18; at the time of this writing, the most recent archive release, *Live 1966*, included 36, for a total of 76 CDs.

To place that into perspective, the 2016 box set comprising Elvis's *entire* album output between his debut and his death demanded only 60 CDs, while that of all Dylan's "regular" albums required just 47.

The sheer variety of Dylan's entire *oeuvre*, of course, has made it easy for many collectors to specialize in just one era: his early years aboard the folk boom; the so-called "electric" age, following his revolutionary 1965 Newport Folk Festival showing....

It is true that few people have ever zeroed in on his early 1970s output; as fan and collector Chris Bentley laughingly put it, "Nobody even *remembers* how bad Dylan was in the early 1970s. No matter that his performance at the Isle of Wight festival in 1970 was widely regarded as triumphant... it was his first gig in four years, people were hardly likely to say anything else.

"But the albums that followed, *Self Portrait, New Morning, Dylan* and the *Pat Garrett* soundtrack, were so disappointing that, when he got back with the Band in 1974, it was so good to hear Dylan at least firing on a few cylinders that even cynics were prepared to overlook the fact that there were only two or three decent songs on the *Planet Waves*: 'Dirge,' 'Going Going Gone' and, if you insist, 'Forever Young.'"

Then came the tour that spawned the *Before The Flood* live album, and the decade was already almost half done and the best Dylan had managed was to tread water. In 1966, his label, Columbia, released Dylan's first *Greatest Hits* collection. In 1971, just five years later, they released his second, *Knocking On Heaven's Door*.

But then the tide turned. First an archive release, *The Basement Tapes*, a double album distillation of the most legendary recording sessions in history, as Dylan and the Band holed up, indeed in a basement in 1967, and jammed their way through every song they could think of.

The collection was flawed, to be sure, but still, there was scarcely a Dylan fan in the world who did not listen to it and perceive the myriad different directions that he could have taken out of the sessions.

Then came *Blood On The Tracks*, a divorce (and more) set to music, and universally proclaimed to be Dylan's greatest album since *Name Your Favorite* a decade or more before. And it still is, from the accusatory snarl of "Tangled Up In Blue," to the aural western "Lily Rosemary and the Jack of Hearts," through "Idiot Wind" and "Simple

Twist Of Fate," and onto the various "alternate versions" that have leaked out onto the collectors' market. As journalist Carol Caffin put it, "This album is a masterpiece, Dylan's magnum opus. It changed my life when I was only fourteen and I have never looked back. Brilliant—a perfect record."

Better was to come. *Desire* may not have been granted the same all-out adoration as its predecessor, but it has just as many high points, and a clutch of songs that even rose above the last album's high bar… the mystifying "Isis," the rollicking "Black Diamond Bay," the plaintive "Sara."

Then came the Rolling Thunder tour, an outing that is almost mythical now, so brilliantly realized was Dylan's medicine show road show; and, although the critics panned *Renaldo and Clara*, the movie that grew so organically from the tour, every time it washed up on the late night theater circuit, the lines stretched around the block.

It's true that Dylan's next album stumbled. 1978's *Street Legal* certainly had its moments—both "Senor (Tales of Yankee Power)" and the opening "Changing of the Guard" would have beautified either of its predecessors, and when Patti Smith covered the latter on her *Twelve* album, she knew exactly what she was doing. Smith is already enshrined in rock history as one of Dylan's biggest fans, and she had his entire career to choose from. She chose "Changing of the Guard." End of discussion.

Neither did Dylan slow down. Between the late 1970s and the early 1990s, Dylan either achieved, or embarked upon some of the most crucial adventures of his entire career, not to mention some of his most astonishing moves—his then-controversial conversion to Born Again Christianity; partnerships with some of the most seminal musicians of the day, from Mark Knopfler and Sly & Robbie, to Keith Richard and Ronnie Wood; groundbreaking, record-smashing tours and collaborations with the Grateful Dead and Tom Petty and the Heartbreakers.

It includes his involvement in the Travelling Wilbury's, perhaps the most misunderstood super group of all time—for who could truly get a handle on a new group fronted by… Dylan, George Harrison, Jeff Lynne and Roy Orbison? His dalliance with reggae, his return to protest music, his reiteration of folk, his sudden love of pop and rock; and the now-legendary and still-churning Never Ending Tour, kicked off in the early nineties and still going strong today. And, most recently, his Nobel Prize and his first triple album, so aptly titled *Triplicate*.

Good choices, bad choices, brilliant notions and crazy conceits—Dylan indulged in all of these, and he still had time to write and record what hindsight now reveals to be some of the most intriguing, inspiring and collected music of the decade and beyond.

CHAPTER 12

MOTOWN: AMERICA'S POP

THE MAJORITY OF PEOPLE WHO collect Motown do so *not* because they love great funk, R&B, soul and disco. Nor are they tireless connoisseurs of Lionel Ritchie, Diana Ross, Steve Wonder and the Jackson Five.

They do so because, more than any single label (or, more accurately, family of labels) in rock history, Motown *is* American pop music, forged in the splendor of the sixties age of discovery and adventure, and redolent still of every hope, dream and aspiration that the country experienced during those years.

Other bands, The Beatles most of all, could be said to have zapped the zeitgeist of the age. But Motown *created* that zeitgeist, and the means by which it could be zapped, in the first place. And when you play through the first few Beatles albums, whose songs ring loudest from the Merseybeat brew? Smokey Robinson ("You Really Got a Hold On Me"), Barrett Strong ("Money"), the Marvelettes ("Please Mr. Postman").

Berry Gordy Jr. founded Motown in 1960, forever changing the sound of Pop music.
Associated Press

Of course other artists placed compositions on those records, from Chuck Berry to Carl Perkins, Arthur Alexander to Larry Williams.

But those artists' songs were already common currency on the beat scenes of Hamburg and Liverpool, where The Beatles learned their trade, and already oldies as well. The Motown sound was something else; the Motown sound was something new; and if all this praise seems subjective (at best) or hyperbolic (at worst), then wait up just one more moment.

For any reader who doesn't happen to have a collection of every Motown 45 released through the sixties alongside them, a sprawling collection of recent CD box sets will take all the strain out of struggling to find them, and line the whole lot up for you to hear.

Some are good, some are bad. Some were hits, some were turkeys. And some are so mind-bogglingly brilliant that you suddenly understand how Lennon and McCartney wrote so many great songs of their own. Because Motown was the role model upon which they based their dreams.

No single artist epitomizes the label. Yes, it had its superstars—the Supremes and the Miracles, Stevie Wonder and Marvin Gaye, the names that became the most reliable hit-makers.

But just as many great records sprang from what we now tend to think of as one, or maybe two hit wonders. Records like, indeed, the Marvelettes' "Please Mr. Postman," Mary Wells' "My Guy," the Elgins' "Heaven Must Have Sent You," Junior Walker's "Roadrunner." And so many, many more that simply listing them

MARVIN
Tamla Recor

One of Motown's biggest stars, Marvin Gaye
Image courtesy Heritage Auctions

makes you want to go and listen.

It was the in-house musicians who played on the records, the in-house producers who made them, the in-house writers who composed them.

Check the credits on a pile of Motown albums and the same names leap out at you again and again—Norman Whitfield, Eddie and Brian Holland, Lamont Dozier, Barrett Strong, Willie Stevenson… and one name leaps out ahead of even them; Berry Gordy Jr., the man whose vision Motown was, and whose demands and determination kept it at the top of the heap for so many years.

Gordy was already renowned as a songwriter and producer when he launched Motown, and had stepped into music publishing too, forming his Jobete house in 1958.

The following January, with a loan of $800, he opened Tamla Records and released the record from which all else would grow. Marv Johnson's "Come to Me" 45 (Tamla 101) was not a hit, but it did attract the attention of the United Artists label. They signed Johnson to a long term deal, hired Gordy as his producer, and their very next effort, "You Got What It Takes" (UA 0030) became Gordy's first Top 10 smash.

A second label, Motown, launched with the Miracles opening its account; their debut "Bad Girl" (TLX 2207) promptly earned them a deal with Chess, again with Gordy in the producer's chair, and the little label was off and running.

By the time Gordy's sister Anna rereleased Barrett Strong's "Money" (Tamla 54027) on her own eponymous label, it was clear that a new force was moving onto the pop scene; and, by the time "Money" made the national Top Thirty, it was apparent that Detroit had itself a brand new suburb. It was called Hitsville.

Collecting Motown is not a pursuit for the faint-hearted. Even concentrating one's attentions on a single act, or even a single year, will leave you with mountains to climb and oceans to swim.

There was no single label to pursue. The Tamla and Motown labels were the company's best-known identities (in the UK and Europe, in fact, the entire operation was conducted beneath the single Tamla Motown logo), but other identities proliferated in the US: Check-Mate and Miracle Records launched in 1961 (and closed shortly thereafter); Gordy and the short-lived Workshop Jazz were birthed in 1962; Soul and VIP in 1964. And all three of these latter concerns flourished—VIP until 1974 and Soul until 1978, while Gordy survived until as late as 1988.

Other subsidiaries (Rare Earth, MoWest, Motown Yesteryear and more) would follow in the years and decades to come, and all had their own rosters of artists, all operated their own catalog numbering system... and all (with the possible exception of Rare Earth, which was Gordy's attempt to break into the rock market) rejoiced beneath the glorious singularity of the Motown Sound.

Specialize in collecting one subsidiary and you miss out on all the greatness that came out on the others; attempt to collect them all, and you have a full-time job.

Those aforementioned CD box sets give the beginner some idea of what is in store. Available both in individual volumes devoted to single years , or as an all-consuming box set, no less than seventy-five disc round up a- and b-sides of every 45 the Motown conglomerate released from its birth until 1972. By comparison, a similar venture by the Stax-Volt family—Motown's only real competitor throughout its golden years—was able to cram its entire sixties singles catalog onto nine. *The Complete Motown Singles*

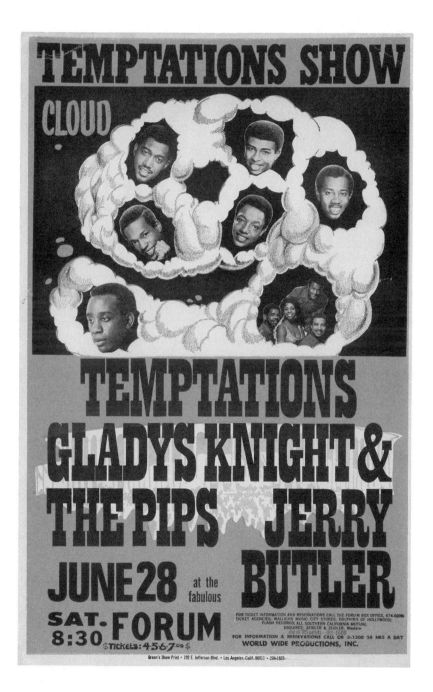

25 ELUSIVE MOTOWN ALBUMS
1961-1969

Mary Wells: *The One Who Really Loves You* (Motown M605, 1962) current value: **$160**

Various artists: *Motown Special* (Motown M603, 1962) current value: **$100**

Martha & the Vandellas: *Come and Get These Memories* (Gordy G-902, 1963) current value: **$400**

Choker Campbell: *Hits of the Sixties* (Motown M-620, 1964) current value: **$150**

Marvin Gaye & Mary Wells: *Together* (Motown M613, 1964) current value: **$50**

Mary Wells: *The One Who Really Loves You* (Motown M605, 1964) current value: **$40**

Martha & the Vandellas: *Dance Party* (Gordy GS-915, 1965) current value: **$75**

Jr. Walker & the All Stars: *Soul Session* (Soul 702, 1966) current value: **$75**

Isley Brothers: *This Old Heart of Mine* (Tamla T-269, 1966) current value: **$30**

Barbara McNair: *Here I Am* (Motown 644, 1966) current value: **$50**

Chris Clark: *Soul Sounds* (Motown M-664, 1967) current value: **$50**

Chuck Jackson: *...Arrives!*
(Motown MS-667, 1967)
current value: **$30**

The Spinners; *The Original
Spinners* (Motown M639, 1967)
current value: **$30**

Jimmy Ruffin: *Top Ten* (Soul
S-704, 1967) current value: **$30**

Shorty Long: *Here Comes
the Judge* (Soul SS-709, 1968)
current value: **$25**

Gladys Knight & the Pips:
Feelin' Bluesy (Soul S707, 1968)
current value: **$40**

Edwin Starr: *Soul Master*
(Gordy GS-931, 1968) current value: **$30**

**Bobby Taylor and the
Vancouvers:** *Bobby Taylor
and the Vancouvers* (Gordy
G-930, 1968) current value: **$100**

Edwin Starr: *25 Miles* (Gordy
GS-940, 1969) current value: **$30**

Jimmy Ruffin: *Ruff'n Ready*
(Soul S-708, 1969) current value: **$30**

Gladys Knight & the Pips:
Nitty Gritty (Soul SS713, 1969)
current value: **$30**

The Fantastic Four: *The Best
of...:* (Soul SS-717, 1969)
current value: **$40**

Shorty Long: *The Prime of...*
(Soul SS-719, 1969) current value: **$18**

The Monitors: *Greetings,
We're the Monitors* (Soul SS-
714, 1969) current value: **$75**

The Originals: *Baby I'm for
Real* (Soul SS-716, 1969)
current value: **$40**

Collection is exactly what it says.

But come on, where's the fun in simply buying a bunch of compact discs and pretending you have what you set out to collect? CDs are great for filling in the gaps in the collection, or lining up to play in a continuous sequence... try that with the original singles and you'll have jumped up to flip or change the record almost 150 times before you're even out of 1962. Multiply that by the rest of the catalog and you could probably cancel your gym subscription right now.

Yet singles are the optimum medium for the Motown experience. The deepest secrets of the label's production techniques remain closely guarded, and so they should. But nobody else, not even Phil Spector, was able to capture that precise sound on vinyl, a noise that felt as good coming out of a tiny transistor radio or the boxiest mono record player, as it did from the greatest sound system on the planet.

Indeed, some quite remarkable rumors flew—including the belief that Motown's UK operation recorded its masters direct from Detroit by trans-Atlantic telephone! One very much doubts that the story is true, but it does convey a sense of the sheer excitement and immediacy that those singles possessed.

Nevertheless, for all its glory, the Motown family's 45s tell only a part of the story. The label commenced issuing albums in 1961, with the Miracles' *Hi... We're the Miracles* (TM 220) debuting the Tamla subsidiary, and Mary Wells' *Bye, Bye Baby/I Don't Want to Take a Chance* (MLP 600).

Both remain fabulous listens; both set the stage for so much of what was to come—1961 saw Marvin Gaye take his long-playing bow; 1962 introduced the Supremes and Little Stevie Wonder to the family; 1963 brought Martha and the Vandellas into the spotlight; 1964 brought long playing debuts from the Four Tops and the Temptations and in 1965, Junior Walker and the All Stars unveiled the almighty *Shotgun...* and those acts, of course, are simply the very best known in a catalog that already topped 100 long-played releases.

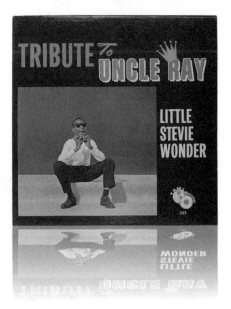

Like their seven-inch

cousins, Motown albums were both hit and miss in the contemporary marketplace, and the collector's world reflects that. Dollar bins across the country ache beneath the weight of sundry Supremes, Temptations and Four Tops albums, with the Miracles close behind them.

Stevie Wonder and Marvin Gaye do tend to attract slightly higher prices in even the most lamentable condition, alongside what we might describe as the second wave of Motown superstars, the generation that began emerging during 1967-1968 forming a new tier of their own—the Isley Brothers (already established superstars elsewhere, of course), Jimmy and David Ruffin, Edwin Starr and forth.

If a collector truly doesn't care any more for condition than that a record should play through without too many skips or surface noise, a sizable sixties Motown collection could readily be obtained for under $100; more discerning ears could muster a similar collection in at least VG+ for around a grand.

It's when you move out of those waters that the true challenge of Motown collecting becomes apparent—not always in the cost of things, but simply in finding them in the first place.

Many of the albums (the Soul label is especially guilty of this) you'll be chasing are certainly out there, and they're not especially costly, either. But you can scour the racks, and the Internet too, for months... even years... in search of a certain something (believe me, I've tried), and invariably wind up disappointed.

And when you finally graduate to the upper tier, to those albums that even lifelong collectors sometimes despair of finding in acceptable condition, you begin to wonder whether or not you will ever "complete" the collection.

Of course, this is true no matter what you are collecting, be it music, books, fossils or historic weather forecasts. There's always a holy grail that glistens just out of sight; there's always the break in the sequence that can drive you to utter distraction if you only think about it enough.

Few of them, however, sound as great as a missing Motown album— and how do you know that? Because they almost all sound great. Because they're Motown.

YOU WANT TO KNOW A SECRET?

HOW TO COLLECT THE BEATLES

FORGET THE FACT THAT THEY were fantastic. Forget that they revolution-ized rock, and wrote some of the most successful songs of all time. It is more than 50 years… and will soon be 60… since The Beatles first emerged on the music scene; it is, in fact, 60-plus years since John, Paul and George recorded their first songs together. And that's a long time in rock music.

Travel back half a century from when The Beatles released their first hit single, "Love Me Do," in the UK in 1962. The biggest hits in America in 1912 were still being tabulated from sheet music sales, meaning people weren't even bothering with pop stars and singers, because they were playing the songs themselves!

The idea that the Fab Four-to-be, or any other contemporary beat group, might have bonded over a mutual love of "Down On The Farm" by Raymond A. Brown and Harry Tilzer, "The Face in the Firelight" by Charles Shackford, or even "The Entertainer" by Scott Joplin (reborn in the seventies as the theme to Robert Redford and Paul Newman academy-award winning movie, *The Sting*) is beyond absurd.

But that is how all-pervading The Beatles are, because today, young bands still form with a strong Beatles influence, and young collectors still get their

For the record, The Beatles remain popular.
Image courtesy of Julien's Auctions

start hunting down the band's old records, most of which were already ancient when their own parents were born.

Rock 'n' roll was born as music for kids, a rebellious outpouring of angst and excitement that not only widened, but also positively *created* the generation gap of the sixties and beyond. The idea that the kids of one generation would even acknowledge the music of their parents' youth was anathema to all that rock 'n' roll stood for, which is how the punks of the late 1970s got away with calling even their most recent musical predecessors "boring old farts."

But times change, and attitudes too. As the young guns of the sixties crossed the threshold into their thirties—because it *was* a threshold, a dark and foreboding gateway into utterly unknown territory—their fans followed them, and were pleasantly surprised when they did not wake up on that fateful birthday to discover they'd turned into Bing Crosby fans overnight. Their forties followed, their fifties and beyond.

And still the bands rocked on—maybe not with the same conviction as before, and certainly not with the same energy. And some of their earlier, more sexual lyrics did feel a little creepy being uttered by a septuagenarian with more wrinkles than riffs. But they kept on keeping on, and not only did their original audience follow, so did that audience's kids and grandkids.

The Beatles just kept on more emphatically than most, and that despite having broken up back in 1970 and, unlike so many other survivors from rock's hoary past, never getting back together.

Everything they accomplished, and everything that we love today, they achieved in just eight years of joint activity—eight years, 12 original albums, 13 extended play EPs and 22 singles.

At least, that's what they thought they were releasing, and that's what came out in their British homeland.

Other countries, however, sifted that tally into other quantities entirely, stripping songs from one album and planting them on another; or taking non-LP material and creating whole new collections.

In the United States, Capitol Records transformed those 12 UK albums (the "core catalog," as it is known) into 17, and even that was not a definitive title because, when Capitol

released *Their Second Album*, they ignored the fact that another label, Vee Jay, had already released one as well. So their second was actually their third, and *Beatles VI* (six) was actually *Beatles VIII*, thanks to a handful of recordings that the pre-fame Beatles made in Germany making it out as well. Recent years have seen much of this confusion reigned in by the release, on vinyl and CD, of the entire original "core catalog" as mono and stereo box sets. But step back from the new release racks and into the world of record fairs, and an entire world of possibilities (with a smattering, too, of bewilderment) opens up.

There are a multitude of foreign releases to consider, most of them simply echoing familiar UK or U.S. releases, but occasionally going their own sweet way.

Canada's first Beatles fans, for example, grew up on *Twist and Shout* and *The Beatles Long Tall Sally*; and while neither was released in the U.S., sufficient copies crossed the border to render them so familiar to American collectors that one of the most common queries received at *Goldmine* asks why they're not listed in the *Standard Catalog of American Records*. ("Because they're not American" is the standard response.)

The Beatles catalog is not unique in any of these factors. Most British Invasion bands (and others besides) saw their UK albums shaved and shifted to create brand new American collections; most saw U.S. buyers go nuts for singles that the bands barely knew had been released (those 22 UK Beatles singles became close to 40 over here).

But, more than any of the others, it illustrates the intricacies that a collector

The 45 that helped launch Apple Records in 1968, "Hey Jude" with "Revolution" on the flip side.

is capable of willingly bringing upon him or herself, once the decision has been made to stop simply *buying records*, and start *collecting an artist*.

The parameters to such a collection are all your own, but we'll stick with vinyl here… suffice to say, The Beatles made it onto almost every format that existed in the sixties, including such arcane delights as 4-Track cartridges (forerunners, of course, of 8-Tracks), Playtapes (a short-lived "self winding" tape launched in the mid-1960s), reel-to-reel tapes, 78s and flexi discs.

Indeed, some of the most sought-after flexi discs of all were the work of The Beatles, a series of Christmas offerings produced for their fan club, generally featuring the boys mucking around with a festive flavor, snatches of song and plenty of joking.

As a listening experience, they scarcely rank alongside *Sgt. Pepper* or *Revolver,* but they capture the spirit of unbridled Beatlemania better than many a subsequent book, movie or documentary. As does a fistful of 45s released in tribute to The Beatles, on both sides of the Atlantic, during the first flush of mega-fame. You can file the following under Novelty!

Annie and The Orphans—*My Girl's Been Bitten by the Beatle Bug* (Capitol 5144)

Becky Lee Beck—*Want a Beatle for Christmas* (Challenge 9372)

Christine Hunter—*Santa Bring Me Ringo* (Roulette 4584)

Cindy Rella—*Bring Me a Beatle for Christmas* (Drum Boy 112)

Donna Lynn—*My Boyfriend got a Beatle Haircut* (Capitol 5127)

Dora Bryan—*All I Want for Christmas is a Beatle* (UK Fontana TF 427)

Garry Ferrier—*Ringo-Deer* (Canada Capitol 72202)

Jackie and Jill—*I Want a Beatle for Christmas* (USA 791)

The Fans—*I Want a Beatle for Christmas* (Dot 16688)

The Four Preps—*A Letter To The Beatles* (Capitol 5143)

Tich and Quackers—*Santa Bring Me Ringo* (UK Oriole CB 1980)

The Beatles' own American catalog is, at the same time, both easy and next-to-impossible to collect in its entirety. It's easy if you opt simply for one copy of each album, perhaps focusing in on the earliest affordable pressing you can find, in the best possible condition—and, bearing in mind just how many millions of copies of each album they sold, and how many different releases each has seen, that is scarcely an imposing proposition.

Take, for example, that mistitled *Second Album*, released in 1964 as a combination of recent UK singles and EP tracks, plus tracks drawn from the band's second UK LP, *With The Beatles*.

1964 (Capitol ST-8-2080—Capitol Record Club edition; black label with colorband): **$600**

1964 (Capitol ST2080—stereo): **$150**

1964 (Capitol T2080—mono): **$300**

1968 (Apple/Capitol ST2080—with Capitol logo on Side 2 bottom): **$40**

1968 (Capitol ST2080, 1968—Black colorband label; border print adds "A Subsidiary of Capitol Industries Inc."): **$50**

1969 (Capitol ST-8-2080—Capitol Record Club edition; lime green label): **$400**

1969 (Capitol ST2080—lime green label): **$40**

1971 (Apple/Capitol ST2080—with "Mfd. by Apple" on label): **$25**

1975 (Apple/Capitol ST2080—with "All Rights Reserved" on label): **$30**

1976 (Capitol ST2080—orange label): **$15**

1978 (Capitol ST2080—purple label, large Capitol logo): **$12**

1983 (Capitol ST2080—Black label, print in colorband): **$18**

1988 (Capitol C1-90444—new catalog number; purple label, small Capitol logo): **$30**

All of which is relatively straightforward. But of course it isn't. Not if you start adding further challenges to the quest, by seeking out editions from the different pressing plants that Capitol was utilizing around the country; by seeking out the (admittedly minor) label variations that have been recorded; by pursuing the different matrix numbers scratched into the dead wax. Then multiplying the ensuing quantities by every other available Beatles album. Where The Beatles are concerned, completeness is not a hobby. It's an obsession. And it can prove a very expensive one.

Some of the hobby's greatest rarities are Beatles-related. And they're genuinely rare, as well.

Signed to EMI's Parlophone label in the UK, The Beatles were automatically offered to its counterpart Capitol Records in America.

Capitol turned them down, and so the band's first records were licensed instead to Vee Jay (who handled the U.S. releases by another EMI artist, Frank Ifield). Vee Jay then distributed those early singles across its own subsidiaries, Swan and Tollie, as well as the parent label, and then gathered them together as *Introducing The Beatles*, an album that, on the one hand, feels like it's among the most common Beatles albums of all; and, on the other, is responsible for some of the most sought-after variations.

1964 (Vee Jay SR1062—stereo: advertising on back cover; with "Love Me Do" and "P.S. I Love You" (both mono); oval Vee Jay logo with colorband only): **$12,000**

1964 (Vee Jay SR1062—stereo: song titles cover; with "Love Me Do" and "P.S. I Love You"; oval Vee Jay logo with colorband only. This album has been heavily counterfeited; if the words "Introducing The Beatles" are above the center hole of the record, and "The Beatles" appears below, it is automatically a counterfeit and almost worthless): **$10,000**

1964 (Vee Jay LP1062- mono: advertising on back cover; with "Love Me Do" and "P.S. I Love You"; oval Vee Jay logo with colorband only): **$5,000**

1964 (Vee Jay SR1062—stereo: blank back cover; with "Love Me Do" and "P.S. I Love You"; oval Vee Jay logo with colorband only): **$2,500**

1964 (Vee Jay SR1062—stereo: song titles cover; with "Please Please Me" and "Ask Me Why"; oval Vee Jay logo with colorband): **$1,600**

1964 (Vee Jay SR1062—stereo: song titles cover; with "Please Please Me" and "Ask Me Why"; plain Vee Jay logo on solid black label): **$1,600**

1964 (Vee Jay SR1062- stereo: song titles cover; with "Please Please Me" and "Ask Me Why"; brackets Vee Jay logo with colorband): **$1,500**

1964 (Vee Jay LP1062—mono: blank back cover; with "Love Me Do" and "P.S. I Love You"; oval Vee Jay logo with colorband only): **$1,500**

1964 (Vee Jay LP1062—mono: song titles cover; with "Please Please Me" and "Ask Me Why"; brackets Vee Jay logo on solid black label): **$1,000**

1964 (Vee Jay LP1062—mono: blank back cover; with "Please Please Me" and "Ask Me Why"; oval Vee Jay logo with colorband only): **$1000**

1964 (Vee Jay LP1062—mono: Song titles cover; with "Love Me Do" and "P.S. I Love You"; oval Vee Jay logo with colorband only): **$1,000**

1964 (Vee Jay LP1062—mono: song titles cover; with "Please Please Me" and "Ask Me Why"; oval Vee Jay logo with colorband): **$400**

1964 (Vee Jay LP1062—mono: song titles cover; with "Please Please Me" and "Ask Me Why"; brackets Vee Jay logo with colorband. This is the most common authentic version of this album.): **$300**

1964 (Vee Jay LP1062—mono: song titles cover; with "Please Please Me" and "Ask Me Why"; plain Vee Jay logo on solid black label): **$300**

1964 (Vee Jay LP1062—mono: song titles cover; with "Please Please Me" and "Ask Me Why"; oval Vee Jay logo on solid black label) current value: **$300**

THE BEATLES

PAUL

JOHN

RINGO

GEORGE

The other core Beatles rarity is the so-called Butcher cover.

In 1965, preparing their latest American album *Yesterday and Today*, The Beatles opted for what can best be described as a very striking photograph, by Bob Whitaker, depicting themselves draped with the remnants of sundry dismembered dolls and cuts of meat.

Early into the next decade, Alice Cooper would virtually build a career around such imagery, but even that band drew the line at bloodstains.

Capitol, too, freaked out—but only after 750,000 copies of the record with the offending cover had been shipped to distributors and DJs, and uniformly condemned as tasteless.

So the records were recalled. A new cover depicting the band sedately surrounding a piece of luggage was pasted over the offending butcher cover. Which, to further the Alice Cooper analogy, was advertised in the trade press beneath the slogan "School's Out!"

Hunting down the butcher cover is one of Beatledom's most delightful pursuits. A handful escaped without being doctored— these are referred to as "first state" and are currently valued at $12,000 (stereo) and $4,000 (mono)

"Second state" is a fully obscured butcher cover, pasted over but maybe just revealing a glimpse of its original image: $2,000 (stereo) and $1,500 (mono)

"Third state" has the trunk cover removed, leaving the butcher cover intact, but with signs of the removal apparent. A clean removal is valued at up to $1,500 (stereo) and $1,200 (mono); however, some butcher covers have indeed been butchered by a past owner's attempts to remove the new picture, and their value plunges accordingly.

Indeed, if ever you are offered a third state butcher cover, it is vital that you keep in mind what the original picture looked like, and how much of it can be seen on the specimen you are holding. Even the world's most fabulous rarities are all but worthless if they've been ripped and torn too much. Although the opportunity to own such a genuine piece of Beatles history, and one of the most notorious, too, is a difficult one to resist.

Many people and events have been said to have "changed the world." The Beatles, however, actually did so musically, commercially and culturally, which is why many collectors do not concentrate on the records alone.

Arriving in the United States in early 1964, at a time when the country was still reeling from the assassination of President Kennedy the previous November, The Beatles effectively ushered in what we now think of as "the sixties"—not the literal calendar span, but the cultural insurgence that gifted us with everything from pop art comics to Haight-Asbury hippies, from Swinging London to New Wave cinema, from "Please Please Me" to "Let It Be."

To the teenyboppers, they were idols; to the teens, they were figureheads; to musicians, they were examples; to scholars, they were geniuses. Even grown-ups liked The Beatles and that might have been the most remarkable thing of all.

With such a vast market opening up before them, there descended a plethora of what we might call "related material" to seek out alongside the records, much of it issued during, and again indelibly resonant of, the first years of Beatlemania.

THE BEATLES ON A BUDGET
AFFORDABLE ORIGINAL ALBUMS

Introducing The Beatles (Vee Jay LP1062, 1964—mono: song titles cover; with "Please Please Me" and "Ask Me Why"; brackets Vee Jay logo with colorband): **$300**

Meet The Beatles! (Capitol ST2047, 1964, repressed 1978): **$12**

The Beatle's Second Album (Capitol ST2080, 1964, repressed 1978): **$150**

A Hard Day's Night (Capitol SW-11921, 1064, repressed 1979): **$15**

Something New (Capitol ST2108, 1964, repressed 1978): **$12**

Songs, Pictures and Stories of the Fabulous Beatles (Vee Jay LP1092, 1964—largely spoken word): **$500**

The Beatles' Story (Capitol STBO2222, 1964, repressed 1978—largely spoken word) current value: **$25**

Beatles '65 (Capitol ST2228, 1964, repressed 1978): **$12**

The Early Beatles (Capitol ST2309, 1965, repressed 1978; effectively replaces Introducing..., should you feel so inclined): **$12**

Beatles VI (Capitol ST2358, 1965, repressed 1978): **$12**

Help! (Capitol SMAS2386, 1965, repressed 1978): **$12**

Rubber Soul (Capitol SW2442, 1965, repressed 1978): **$12**

Everything from Beatles board games ("Flip Your Wig" was a particular favorite) to bottles of Beatles perfume. There were Beatles boots and Beatle wigs; toy guitars, bobblehead figures, die-cast toys and candy bars. If The Beatles' name or image could be affixed to a product, then it would be. There are books to read, movies to watch, cards to collect and clothes to wear.

Musically, too, their silence could not still their sound.

Compilation albums that reach back to the days before Beatlemania... their aforementioned German recordings, for example, or their first, failed, audition for the Decca label; live recordings from a packed, but respectful Hamburg club, or the scream-drenched hysteria of the Hollywood Bowl; "best of" and "rest of"... collections of their radio sessions and b-sides; their wildest rock 'n' rollers and their most tender ballads.

In 2000, a gathering of all the band's chart topping singles itself topped the charts all over the world; in the mid-nineties, three volumes of out-takes and oddities, the *Anthology* series, did likewise.

Sixty years after they first recorded together, more than 50 after their first hit record, and more than four decades after The Beatles broke up, John, Paul, George and Ringo remain the most-loved, best-selling, most-influential and most widely collected rock group in history.

Yesterday and Today (Capitol ST2553, 1966, repressed 1978): **$12**

Revolver (Capitol SW2576, 1966, repressed 1978): **$12**

Sgt. Pepper's Lonely Hearts Club Band (Capitol SMAS2653, 1967, repressed 1978) current value: **$12**

Magical Mystery Tour (Capitol SMAL2835, 1967, repressed 1978): **$12**

The Beatles (Capitol SWBO-101, 1968, repressed 1978): **$30**

Yellow Submarine (Capitol SW-153, 1969, repressed 1978): **$12**

Abbey Road (Capitol SO-383, 1969, repressed 1978): **$12**

Hey Jude (Capitol SW-385, 1970, repressed 1978) current value: **$12**

Circa 1960: In the Beginning featuring Tony Sheridan (Polydor PD-4504, 1970, repressed 1981): **$15**

Let It Be (Capitol SW-11922, 1970, repressed 1978): **$18**

The Beatles at the Hollywood Bowl (Capitol SMAS-11638, 1977, repressed 1980): **$18**

Live at the BBC (Apple C1-8-31796, 1994): **$100**

Anthology 1 (Apple C1-8-34445, 1995): **$175**

Anthology 2 (Apple C1-8-34448, 1996): **$140**

Anthology 3 (Apple C1-8-34451, 1996): **$130**

On Air: Live at the BBC volume two (Apple 3750506, 0602537505067, 2013): **$50**

In the battle of the bands, the Rolling Stones successfully played the bad-boy role.
Image courtesy Heritage Auctions

ROLLING WITH THE STONES

(WERE THEY BETTER THAN THE BEATLES?)

COLLECTING RECORDS IS NOT SIMPLY a matter of ticking boxes alongside the discography, and accumulating a pile of wax that follows a band from beginning to end.

It is also a social study, a private excursion into a period of time that can not only be relived through the music of the moment, but for the attitudes and arguments which that music stood for.

The music of the Vietnam era tells the story of an entire nation riven by a conflict on the other side of the world. A British punk collection illustrates the cultural divides that rent British society in the late 1970s.

And then there's the greatest battle of the bands in history, the war between good and evil set to the pounding beat of rock 'n' roll.

Are you a Beatle or a Rolling Stone?

The Rolling Stones—or, at least, Mick Jagger and Keith Richard—rank among the most important songwriters in rock history. Ever since the night manager Andrew Loog Oldham locked the band's vocalist and guitarist in the kitchen of the flat they shared, and refused to let them out until they'd written their first song, Jagger/Richard has become one of the most successful, and productive songwriting partnerships around, up there with

Rodgers and Hammerstein, Lieber and Stoller and Lennon and McCartney in the pantheon of greats.

Even today, more than five decades after the Stones first started rolling, the first thing anyone looks for on a new Stones album is the latest classic to pour from their pens. The amazing thing is, they almost always find at least one.

Yet it wasn't always like that. For more than a year after the Stones recorded their first single, a savage version of Chuck Berry's "Come On" in 1963... 18 months before the key turned in the kitchen lock that fateful evening... the Stones not only looked elsewhere for their songs, they never even dreamed that there was an alternative.

At least three of the five original band members—Jagger, Richard and Brian Jones—were brought up on Chicago blues, and turned to their treasured Chess and Checker LPs for the inspiration which would see them through another round of recording sessions. It's no coincidence at all that their 2016 album *Blue and Lonesome* drew upon this same wellspring of music for its contents. The band had simply turned full circle.

But, though these urban yowls were the first raw ingredients of the Stones' musical stew, they were never alone in the cauldron for long.

The group were also obsessed with R&B, not only the mood of it but also the feel—"I've Been Loving You Too Long" and "If You Need Me" both catch the Stones going full tilt for an authentic sound, at a time when most white English bands still thought "soul" was a kind of flatfish; while the band demonstrated their taste for eclecticism when they elected to cover the Drifters' "Under The Boardwalk."

Motown, too, was a vibrant influence and, long after Jagger/ Richard began penning their own material, they were still turning to the Motor City library: "My Girl," a hit for the Temptations, was recorded in 1966; and the Miracles' "Going To A Go Go" gave the Stones a Top 30 hit in 1982.

That was the Stones' first hit cover in 18 years. Back at the outset of their career, however, their first five British singles were written elsewhere: after Berry, they visited the Beatles ("I Wanna Be Your Man"), Buddy Holly ("Not Fade Away") and Bobby Womack ("It's All Over Now"), before creating what was arguably their greatest statement yet, a slow, simmering invocation of Howlin' Wolf's "Little Red Rooster."

Like a skilled motor mechanic, they stripped the song down to its barest bones. Unlike a mechanic, they then left it like that, but drove it through the chart regardless. If they'd never actually written a line of original music themselves, their skill as re-arrangers would have ensured their immortality regardless.

The sixties belonged to The Beatles. In every arena one could imagine, from record sales to bums on seats, from posters on the wall to faces on the box, The Beatles dominated musical—and popular—culture in a manner that had never been seen before—and will never be seen again.

But one band chased them every step of the way; one band hung so closely to their footsteps that The Beatles had no choice but to keep on pushing themselves forward. For, if they lagged back for even a moment, they knew they'd fall behind.

That band was the Rolling Stones.

In terms of chart honors, the Stones rarely rattled The Beatles' cage. Their Trans-Atlantic tally of 12 sixties chart-toppers might include five consecutive British #1s, but cannot compete with The Beatles' total of 20. Equally damning, between 1962 and 1970, The Beatles clocked up an amazing 346 weeks on the British chart. It took the Stones until 1994 to finally overhaul that total.

Chart statistics, however, tell only a small part of the story. In terms of personality, adulation and newsworthiness, the Stones had The Beatles matched fiber for fiber, bone for bone and, it seemed, die-hard fan for die-hard fan.

Indeed, when the Stones beat out The Beatles in the "Best British band" section of *Melody Maker*'s 1964 Readers Poll, the *Los Angeles Times* had no hesitation in announcing, "Beatles no longer Number One in British Polls"—and that despite the Fabs scooping both the Best International Band (the Stones finished second) and Top Male Vocalist (Mick Jagger was third) sections.

In terms of actual musical creativity, too, the contest was so close that, even today, fans are still at odds over the untold contributions the two bands made, not only debating who was best, but also who did what first?

The Beatles should win that contest hands down. In career-long producer George Martin, after all, they had a man who possessed more musical knowledge in his little toe than the Stones and their associates had accumulated in their entire bodies.

But that could also work to their disadvantage, as Martin himself admitted on occasion. Faced with a Beatle making a musical suggestion, Martin would know instinctively whether or not it would work, and would guide his charges accordingly. When a Stone came up with a strange idea, their only option was to try it and see. Then, if they liked the way it sounded at the end, into the mix it would go.

Of course, the Beatles did not always heed his master's voice. Particularly during the *Revolver/Sgt. Pepper* era, Beatles lore abounds with occasions when Martin's counsel would be politely ignored, and their sonic legacy grew a little bit larger because of it.

Stones producer/manager Andrew Loog Oldham, on the other hand, speaks for 40 years worth of devotees when he offers up gratitude that, from the head of Decca Records all the way to the kid on the street, "there was *never* anybody there to tell us what we could or couldn't do."

So they did everything they could think of, and it is no coincidence whatsoever that the first time the Stones took control of their own recorded destiny, following Oldham's ouster early into the sessions for 1967's *Their Satanic Majesties Request* LP, it was also the first time that even the most blinkered fan was forced to concede that they were simply following the Beatles' *Sgt. Pepper*-shaped lead.

Prior to that, the only influence that the Beatles had on the Stones' studio output was to show them what they shouldn't be doing. "If they'd already done it, that was it, it had been done," reflects Oldham. "We wanted to do things that hadn't been done."

In reality, of course, the two bands were firm friends. Oldham himself worked as The Beatles' own publicist during 1963, handling the press for "From Me To You" and scoring something of a coup when he landed the band in *Vogue* magazine, the first pop group ever to grace those hallowed pages.

He even tried to interest Brian Epstein in co-managing the Stones when he first took over the band's career and, though Epstein turned him down, The Beatles themselves were always close at hand.

Individually and collectively, the quartet attended the Stones' London concerts, sang their praises in the music press, and was constantly socializing with them on the Swinging London scene. They even wrote their second record for them.

If the public image was of Beatles versus beasties, two bands locked in a no-holds-barred grapple for the heart and mind of sixties pop, the private picture is of a crowded table at the Ad Lib or the Scotch of St. James, the primo watering holes of the Carnaby Street set.

In his *Phelge's Stones* memoir, James Phelge—Jagger, Richards and Jones' flat mate during their early days of poverty—recalled, "an unspoken pecking order determined who sat where, [and] the first three or four tables on the right as you entered [the Ad Lib] had become the natural preserve of the Beatles or the Stones," the two sets of musicians holding joint court and howling over the latest "Ringo Slams Bill"-style tabloid tattle to push reality off the newspaper front pages.

Neither would band or management have had it any other way. Almost from the outset, Oldham's vision was of the Rolling Stones as rivals to The Beatles—with the key word there being "rival." Other groups, The Dave Clark Fives and The Dakotas, The Honeycombs and Herman's Hermits, might have dreamed of some day eclipsing The Beatles, outselling their singles, out-screaming their audience and out-banking their accountants.

But such a vainglorious scenario never even crossed Oldham's mind. He simply wanted to equal the Beatles, step for step, hit for hit—and the foundation stone of his subsequent legend and genius is the fact that he did it.

It is irrelevant to ponder whether or not the Stones would have existed had Oldham not hauled them out of blues club obscurity in summer, 1963. One thing's for certain, though. The Beatles would have had one less thing to worry about if he hadn't.

Oldham lay out his game plan at his first ever official meeting with Stones, at partner Eric Easton's Regent Street offices less than two weeks after he first caught sight of the group, at the Station Hotel in Richmond.

First he outlined everything that was great about the Beatles, and then he detailed the one flaw in their armor. "The public will demand an opposite. For every kid who wants to take the Beatles home, there's another who doesn't want to share." The Stones, he determined, would be the voice of that dissent.

The Stones, for their part, were more than happy to play devils to the Beatles' angels.

Introducing the Beatles at their induction into the Rock 'n' Roll Hall of Fame in 1988, Mick Jagger remembered, "when the Stones were first together, we heard there was a group from Liverpool with long hair, scruffy clothes and a record in the charts with a bluesy harmonica riff. And the combination of all this made me sick." The Stones, he knew, had even longer hair, wore even scruffier clothes, and made The Beatles' blues sound positively pastel by comparison.

Now, here was a fast-thinking and even faster-acting manager, who didn't simply share that viewpoint, he was prepared to live his life according to it. As journalist Don Nicholl put it in the weekly pop paper *Disc*, "the Beatles… may well live to rue the day [they ever met the Stones]. This group could be

The Rolling Stones Lo.

THE ROLLING STONES
THE HIGHEST VALUES
FOR THE HOTTEST HITS

I Wanna Be Your Man/Stoned
(London 9641, 1964): **$9,000**

*She's a Rainbow/2,000 Light Years
from Home//In Another Land/
Citadel/2000 Man* (jukebox issue, small
hole, 33rpm) (London SBG 54, 1967): **$5,000**

*Beast of Burden/When the Whip Comes
Down* (picture sleeve with 1/2-inch inner fold
on the inside of the picture sleeve—beware
counterfeits) (Rolling Stones 19309, 1978):
$2,000

Not Fade Away/I Wanna Be Your Man
(promo white label, two varieties)
(London 9657, 1964): **$1,000**

Heart of Stone/What a Shame
(picture sleeve) (London 9725, 1964): **$800**

We Love You/Dandelion (picture sleeve)
(London 905, 1967): **$600**

*(I Can't Get No) Satisfaction/The Under
Assistant West Coast Promotion Man*
(picture sleeve)(London 9766, 1965): **$500**

Not Fade Away/I Wanna Be Your Man
(picture sleeve) (London 9657, 1964): **$450**

*Around and Around/2120 South
Michigan Avenue/Confessin' the
Blues//Time Is On My Side/Grown
Up Wrong/It's All Over Now*
(London SBG23, 1964): **$275**

*Down the Road Apiece/Off the Hook/Oh
Baby* (We Got a Good Thing Goin')/Everybody
Needs Somebody to Love/Heart of Stone/
Surprise, Surprise (London SBG34, 1965): **$250**

*The Spider and the Fly/One More Try/
Hitch Hike//The Last Time/Good
Times/Mercy Mercy* (London SBG37,
1965): **$250**

*Talkin' 'Bout You/Look What You've
Done/Get Off of My Cloud//I'm
Free/Gotta Get Away/As Tears Go By*
(London SBG43, 1965): **$250**

Far Away Eyes (same on both sides) (Rolling
Stones 19307, 1978): **$250**

The Last Time/Play with Fire (picture
sleeve) (London 9741, 1965): **$200**

We Love You/Dandelion (With 3:10 edited
version of "We Love You"; orange swirl label)
(London 905, 1967): **$200**

Fool to Cry/Hot Stuff (Rolling Stones 19304,
1976): **$200**

Time Waits for No One (mono/stereo) (picture
sleeve)(Rolling Stones PR228, 1974): **$175**

Tell Me (You're Coming Back)/I Just Want to
Make Love to You (picture sleeve) (London 9682,
1964): **$175**

It's All Over Now/Good Times, Bad Times
(picture sleeve) (London 9687, 1964): **$125**

Time Is On My Side/Congratulations
(picture sleeve) (London 9708, 1964): **$125**

19th Nervous Breakdown/Sad Day
(orange swirl label) (London 9823, 1966): **$100**

Exile on Main Street (7-inch EP)
(Rolling Stones COC 7-22900, 1972): **$100**

Goats Head Soup (7-inch EP) (Rolling Stones
CO7-59101, 1973): **$100**

*Rip This Joint/Hip Shake/Tumbling
Dice//Rocks Off/Sweet Virginia*
(Rolling Stones COC 7-22900, 1972): **$100**

*Star Star/Hide Your Love//Can You Hear
the Music/100 Years Ago* (Rolling Stones
CO7-59101, 1973): **$100**

challenging them for top places in the immediate future."

The enemy was targeted, the battle plans were drawn. Now all the Stones needed do was rope in the orchestra that would pluck the strings of the Stone-age rebellion—indignant retired military men who couldn't believe that they'd fought umpteen world wars for the sake of this long-haired rabble; outraged government ministers who saw in pop's unkempt visage all the failings of the opposing party's past *prima-donna* policies; mortified mums and disgusted dads, horrified hairdressers and grumbling grannies, anyone and everyone who could look at an 8 x 10 of Mick Jagger's rubber lips, Brian Jones' lecherous leer, Keith Richard's gypsy skeleton, and send a fervent prayer to Heaven… "dear God, please let the Russians come to town before the Rolling Stones get here."

A gifted promo man long before he ever set foot in the recording studio (an auspicious date that ultimately produced the first Stones single, "Come On") Oldham stoked the outrage with tireless guile.

Feeding the newspapers every morsel he could find, wrapping the tiniest tidbit in tenderloin taste to ensure that, no matter how well-stuffed the fury grew, it would always be salivating for a mouthful more, he recalls his mission to "embed the Stones in the psyche of the British press, like a grain of sand irritates an oyster. I was relentless and I was right. I was like a pit-bull terrier that won't let go. I got a lot of permanent messages across, a lot of press and a lot of enemies."

The Stones' very existence was like a banquet before a starving man. Where the Beatles were smart, the Stones were scruffy. Where The Beatles were cuddly, the Stones were rough. Where the Beatles promised a goodnight peck, the Stones threatened an all-night orgy. And, while the Beatles made cheeky jokes to royalty, the Stones urinated on filling station walls. Clean pop's Jekyll had met his unwashed rocker Hyde, and neither band would ever be the same again.

Even within the world of pop music, such a vivid contrast was a novelty. There had, of course, been rivalries in the past—rock 'n' roll was barely born before its putative founder, Bill Haley, was being challenged by a host of young upstarts, while King Elvis himself had scarcely been crowned before he was back on deck to repel incoming boarders.

But those tussles were different, mere marketing moves that had no more significance than a blackbird's belch or a hamster's ghost. What Andrew Oldham was proposing, and what the Stones themselves represented, was a clash of cultures, of lifestyles, of tradition itself. In the white corner, the Beatles, heirs apparent to an age-old lineage of cheerful family entertainers, with toe-tapping tunes and cheeky, winning grins. And in the black corner, the most Neanderthal demons that Satan could spare.

Like ninepins bowled over by the sheer force of Beatle personality, authorities that should have fallen over themselves to condemn their yowling yeah-yeah-yeah-ing instead rushed to praise it to unimagined heights. Because, now they had seen the alternative—and compared to the Stones, The Beatles sounded like Beethoven.

Even the similarities between the two groups became screaming points of contention. When The Beatles put on suits, they looked like trendy bank clerks, smart young men you could take home to meet your granny. When the Stones put them on, they resembled flashy gangsters who'd take one look at the white-haired old dear, then make off with her pension book.

When the Beatles grew their hair long, they looked poetic, a bunch of little Shelleys. When the Stones unveiled their manes, they looked more like his wife, Mary. And (according to the London *Times*), when the Beatles wrote a new song, it ached with "chains of pan diatonic clusters," or echoed the same "Aeolian cadence…, which ends Mahler's 'Song of the Earth.'" When the Stones came out with a new record, it sounded like Fred Flintstone had just stepped on Dino's toe.

Oldham continues, "I was promoting the idea that the Rolling Stones were 'the group parents loved to hate,' based on my belief that pop idols fall into one of two categories—ones you wished to share with your parents, and ones you did not. The Beatles were accepted and acceptable, they were the benchmark and had set the level of competition. The Stones came to be portrayed as dangerous, dirty and degenerate, and I encouraged [them] to be as nasty as they could wish to be."

Even the conventional music press was opposed to the air of depravity that the Stones wore like an all-enveloping cloak. Echoing all the outrage that would greet punk rock some fifteen years later, *Melody Maker*'s Ray Coleman complained, "they don't wear uniforms, don't need mirrors as they hardly bother with examining themselves before they wander on stage. Hair combing is rare, face make-up unheard of. And they are within striking distance of the big-time."

In an age when even the most respectable little ladies were swearing they'd cut off a leg for the chance to wed (or, at least, bed) a Beatle, Coleman spoke for every brother in the land when he demanded to know, "would you let your sister marry a Rolling Stone?"

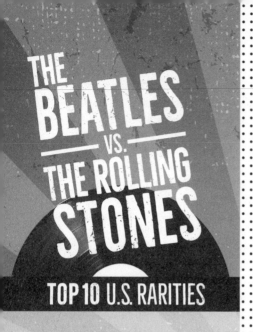

THE BEATLES —VS.— THE ROLLING STONES

TOP 10 U.S. RARITIES

The Rolling Stones: *Street Fighting Man/No Expectations* (picture sleeve) (London 909, 1968): **$15,000**

The Beatles: *Introducing the Beatles* (stereo LP featuring "Love Me Do" and "PS I Love You; ads for other Vee Jay releases on reverse) (Vee Jay SR 1062, 1964): **$12,000**

The Beatles: *Yesterday and Today* (first-state butcher cover) (Capitol ST 2553, 1965): **$12,000**

The Beatles: *Hear the Beatles Tell All* (promo with press release etc.) (Vee Jay PRO202, 1964): **$10,000**

The Rolling Stones: *I Wanna Be Your Man/Stoned* (London 9641, 1964): **$9,000**

The Beatles: *Please Please Me/ From Me to You* (Special The Record That Started Beatlemania promo-only sleeve) (Vee Jay 581, 1964): **$8,000**

The Rolling Stones: *Big Hits* (High Tide and Green Grass) (With two lines of type on the front cover, all in small letters) (London NP1, 1966): **$8,000**

The Beatles: *The Beatles and Frank Ifield Onstage...* (Vee Jay LP1085, 1964): **$6,000**

The Rolling Stones: *Through the Past, Darkly* (Big Hits Vol. 2) (picture disc) (London NPS 3, 1969): **$6,000**

The Rolling Stones: *The Promotional Album* (London RSD-1, 1969): **$5,000**

Neither was the furor confined solely to Britain. In August 1964, in the wake of the Stones' first, short, American tour, *16* magazine placed a finger on the nation's pulse when it asked "Has England gone too far?"

"Write and tell us what YOU think," the headline demanded but, read on and there was no doubting how *16* viewed this latest manifestation of the British Invasion— "sloppy, pallid, unkempt and weird looking."

Mick Jagger, we learned, "went to school at the London School of Economics and used to be considered an 'egghead.' Keith vaguely resembles a brunet English sheepdog. Bill looks like… Abraham Lincoln. Watch out world, here come the Rolling Stones!"

Other writers were equally swift to send their own barbs whistling Stones-wards. Wyman's *Stone Alone* autobiography recalls one New York area story that condemned the Stones for being "shaggier, shabbier and uglier than the Beatles"; and another that opined, "if you think the Beatles are way out, wait till you gander the Stones."

But it was the *Toronto Star* that truly voiced the horror that was now coursing not only through the United States' veins, but those of all of North America, as the Stones prepared to roll across their land.

"Those who think the Beatles

caused too much of an uproar when they arrived here had better take to the bomb-shelters when the Rolling Stones arrive. They are hard to describe. They don't believe in bathing, they wear dirty old clothes, their hair is twice as long as the Beatles' and they never comb it." To put it in a nutshell, these Stones sounded frightful.

By the time of their US debut, of course, the Stones had long since conquered their homeland, with their first major hit—following on from "Come On"'s peak of #21—coming with "I Wanna Be Your Man," a song that pop-pickers of the age were swift to identify as another outpouring of the Beatles' own hit factory.

That, in itself, was nothing unusual—just a year into the limelight, and Lennon/McCartney had already established themselves among the most prolific songwriters of the entire pop era, simply spinning off new songs for anyone who asked.

But those other beneficiaries of the duo's largesse tended to be nice people, old Liverpool friends who shared Brian Epstein's management— Billy J Kramer, Cilla Black, Gerry and the Pacemakers. In other words, they were no competition. The Stones, on the other hand, had made no secret whatsoever of their desire to sink their milky white teeth into The Beatles' fleshy behind.

In 1971, John Lennon played down the importance of "I Wanna Be Your Man," telling *Rolling Stone*, "it was a throwaway. The only two versions of the song were Ringo and the Rolling Stones. We weren't going to give them anything great, right?"

But he spoke with the benefit of six years of hindsight and, of course, sustained success. In autumn 1963, when even the biggest pop group's life had hitherto been measured in months before someone else rode up to sink their battleship, it was scarcely comprehensible that The Beatles would even dream of extending a helping hand to the Stones, let alone actually offer them a song that was clearly Top 20-bound. Do bears carry bandoliers in case the hunter runs out of bullets?

But The Beatles knew what they were doing, just as the Stones knew what they were accepting. "It was a match made in heaven," Oldham reflects. "The north and south of musical life, rampant youth colliding."

In 1965, reacting to the massive success of the Beatles' first two movies, Oldham seriously considered casting the Stones in a movie version of author Dave Wallis' *Only Lovers left Alive*, an apocalyptic novel in which Rebellious Youth rises as one to overthrow the world of the over-thirties. "I Wanna Be Your Man"—the marriage of Beatle pens and Stone voices, Mersey beat and R&B rhythms—was the first stroke towards forging that unity, and transforming that scenario into reality.

Of course, the revolution never happened. While the Stones remained evil incarnate, their mirror image Beatles were just too cute, too clever and way too popular to ever make it as *bona fide* enemies of the people. But the two bands carved the marketplace between them regardless, thrilling onlookers with a sense of rivalry that was so tightly strung that you could cut cheese with it.

In concert, there was nothing in it at all. Wyman's autobiography notes at least two occasions upon which the Stones were booked to open shows for The Beatles and, both times, he records the nervousness with which the headliners witnessed the maniacal response that the Stones whipped up. Normally when the Beatles played, their support acts were inaudible beneath the keening chants of Merseybeat mayhem.

When the Stones opened for them at the Albert Hall, you got the impression that the Fabs could have dropped their trousers on stage, and every eye would still have remained fixed on Mick Jagger. In the words of *16*, "the teenagers of England have gone absolutely bananas over these five fantastic young men." Bananas, with plenty of cream.

Both bands can still be heard in their scream-inducing prime, the Stones via the *Got Live If You Want It* album released in the U.S. in 1966; the Beatles via *Live at the Hollywood Bowl*, recorded the previous year, but unreleased until 1977. And both are more-or-less unlistenable. The screaming swamps everything.

The gap was closing in the stores as well, though, and faster than even the Stones themselves were aware. When Britain's best selling records of 1964 were tabulated, the Stones not only came out on top in the singles listing as "It's All Over Now" easily outsold all three of the Beatles' offerings, their eponymous debut album beat out the challenge of *A Hard Day's Night* in the LP listings.

Indeed, Bill Wyman still remembers the thrill he felt when he heard, on May 23 1964, that "our debut album had replaced The Beatles at the top of the LP charts, a position they had held for eleven months."

It was, he decreed, "our biggest moment since 'Not Fade Away,'" but of course, that novelty would quickly wear off. Over the next two years, The Beatles and the Stones between them would occupy the top of the UK album charts for 79 weeks—30 for the Stones, 49 for the Beatles—with only Bob Dylan (for three weeks) and the soundtrack to *The Sound Of Music* standing between them and absolute domination.

It was a similar tale in America, and that despite the careful British release schedule being utterly skewed by the two bands' respective record companies' own policy of squeezing as many hits out of one album as they possibly could. (In the UK, neither the Stones nor the Beatles featured their hit singles on their LPs; in the U.S., it sometimes felt as though that's all the albums contained.) Throughout 1965, there was a fresh Beatles or Stones single entering the U.S. chart in 10 out of 12 months.

Again, the cumulative figures speak volumes for the strength of the hold the two bands exerted over the nation's record-buying public, and the narrowness of the gulf that divided them.

Between 1964 and 1969, the Stones spent 223 weeks on the American chart. If one overlooks the sheer insanity of 1964 itself, when absolutely anything with The Beatles' name on it entered the U.S. chart (and stayed there for a combined 234 weeks!), the Fab Four mustered 283, a margin that becomes even less impressive when one remembers that the Beatles placed 34 separate sides, spread over 19 singles, on the listings, compared to the Stones' 23 songs, and 20 releases.

Of course, it is difficult to play such games with achievements racked up following The Beatles' demise—indeed, far from simply altering that balance, the legend that has grown up around a group which broke up before most folk under the age of 50 were even born has only enhanced their reputation and their sale-ability.

The Beatles remain the biggest-selling band in rock history; the most-collected band likewise; and the be-all and end-all of pop supremacy.

Though the Stones have now outlasted them by more than five decades to one, still the only marketing mantel that is theirs by divine right remains "the greatest rock 'n' roll band in the world." The Beatles have cornered every other accolade there is.

Yet, like black and white, chalk and cheese, day and night, and Ray and Dave Davies, opposites will always attract and, if you mention the Beatles and their hold on the 1960s, the Rolling Stones cannot help but spring to mind alongside them, their unholy opposite, their evil twin, the dark Revelations to the glow of their Genesis.

In terms of press coverage, the "rivalry" between the two groups lasted no more than two years, and had begun to tarnish even before then. But nobody ever asked if the Monkees were mightier than the Mersey band; no one ever claimed that the Doors rolled harder than the Stones.

Already, the two bands were above such pettiness, had ascended to a plateau where they weren't simply unreachable, they were untouchable, a twin benchmark that not only dominated the remainder of that decade, it has now hung suspended over three generations of rock'n'rolling hopefuls. It will probably still be hanging there for generations more to come.

CHAPTER 15

PSYCHEDELIA—
GETTING YOUR FREAK ON!

PSYCHEDELIA IS THE CATCH-ALL NAME given to the explosion of free- (and freak-) minded music that burst out of the American and British undergrounds in 1966; which flourished throughout the so-called Summer of Love the following year; and then gently receded into the backwaters of the musical consciousness, a permanent adornment to rock's expanding roots.

Once again, one can tie oneself in knots trying to pinpoint the first "truly psychedelic" record ever made. History tends, as is so often the case, to spotlight The Beatles, and certainly "Tomorrow Never Knows," from 1966's *Revolver* album, can stake a mighty claim.

But so can the earliest strivings of a host of San Francisco-area bands— the Grateful Dead, Jefferson Airplane, Quicksilver Messenger Service *et al*; and murmurings from the UK too—the Yardbirds, John's Children, the Smoke (whose "My Friend Jack" never received a US release, but remains one of the era's most inviolable statements) and the Pretty Things.

Whoever started it, by early 1967 "psychedelia" was already percolating into the mainstream, a multi-media mélange of lights and sound, film and fantasy; and, to the joy of a growing community of collectors through the 1970s, a fabulous array of obscure 45s that the world had missed the first

A trippy, psychedelic concert poster for Jimi Hendrix and Jefferson Airplane at the Fillmore Auditorium in San Francisco, 1967.
Image courtesy Heritage Auctions

HE CREAM   ATCO RECORDS   GA

From left, Ginger Baker, Jack Bruce and Eric Clapton of the British rock supergroup Cream.

time around, but which were ripe for the hoarding now.

Throughout that decade, and with increasing enthusiasm in the years since then, psychedelic compilations have delved ever deeper into the archive in search of fresh delights—multi-volume collections with titles such as *Circus Days*, *Electric Psychedelic Sitar Headswirlers*, *Piccadilly Sunshine*, *Rubble* and *The Electric Asylum* rejoice in one-upping one another in the search for new rarities; with many of them set to become as collectible in their own right as the singles they preserve.

It is, it must be confessed, strange that a musical medium that we best associate with side-long freak-outs and psilocybic suites should be most collectible on 45.

Yes, there are many psych albums that fall into the realms of the hobby's greatest finds, including a wealth of self-released albums that appeared in the most limited quantities imaginable, and routinely sell for hundreds of dollars apiece.

But there are many times as many singles—a reminder that, in those days, the majority of record labels still regarded the 45 as the true test of a new band's potential, and not until it had proven itself on the singles chart would it be allowed anywhere near an LP. And the fact is, a lot of the bands failed to do so. Those three-or-four minutes on a solitary seven-inch disc was as far as they were able to travel.

The 20 records that we spotlight below are *not* among the psychedelic arena's most expensive, nor are they among the most obscure. Rather, they have been selected from the massed ranks of British psychedelia, to illustrate the sheer range of talent and sound that fell, and still falls, into the genre's catchment area.

Pink Floyd: *See Emily Play/Scarecrow* (Tower 356, 1967): **$200**
The band's second UK hit still resonates almost five decades after founder Syd Barrett wrote it, a dreamy slice of psych pop that was to soundtrack both the Summer of Love and all that nostalgia has added to the era.

The sheer popularity of Pink Floyd among collectors is largely responsible for the price of this single, and limited edition reissues for Record Store Day and within the band's 2016 *Early Years* box set are themselves already soaring in price.

The Herd: *From The Underworld/Sweet William* (Fontana 1602, 1967): **$10**
Vocalist Peter Frampton was voted The Face of '68, seven years before he came alive as the darling of mid-70s' America. Pure pop in dark, moody clothing, "From The Underworld" was the band's only real UK hit, and the Face of 1968 was forgotten by 1969.

Tyrannosaurus Rex: *Debora/Child Star*
(A&M 955, 1968): **$100**
Marc Bolan eventually truncated his band's name to T Rex, and became the biggest British pop star since the height of Beatlemania. Catching him two years before he made the transition from acoustic whimsy to electric attack, "Debora" arrives with all Bolan's lyrical baggage intact, at the same time foreshadowing everything he would achieve musically in the early 1970s.

Julie Driscoll/Brian Auger Trinity: *This Wheel's On Fire/A Kind of Love In* (Atco 6593, 1968): **$20**

As Dylan's unreleased *Basement Tapes* did the UK rounds, any number of would-be pop stars culled the most likely hits from the skeletal demos. Auger, the man who singlehandedly created the jazz-rock fusion of future years, opted for one of the less likely ones, and the combination of his swirling Hammond and the walking bass saw the Trinity hit the UK Top 10 for the first and (criminally) only time.

Cream: *Anyone For Tennis/Pressed Rat and Warthog* (Atco 6575, 1968): **$25**

The archetypal supergroup power trio were always more Blues than blocked, but this ode to Absolutely Nothing rocketed out of a no-man's land that "Crossroads" fans could never envision, and provided rock 'n' roll with one of its most evocative choruses ever, "the elephants are dancing on the brains of squealing mice...." The b-side, "Pressed Rat and Warthog" is worthy of equal attention.

Troggs: *Night of the Long Grass/Girl in Black* (Fontana 1593, 1967): **$8**

"Wild Thing" rockers the Troggs probably couldn't even spell "psychedelia" when they tripped over their first rainbow. And vocalist Reg Presley maintained that impression when he was told you would have to be on drugs to write some of the lyrics he was now coming up with. "Naah," he replied. "You just *pretend* you're on drugs."

Status Quo: *Pictures Of Matchstick Men/Gentleman Joe's Sidewalk Cafe* (Cadet Concept 7001, 1968): **$10**

Quo eventually became (and remain) a British institute, with almost 50 years of deliberately near-identical barrelhouse boogie-ing to their recorded credit. "Matchstick Men" would come as something of a shock to anyone catching them late in the day; fey, whimsical, and delightfully, utterly nonsensical, it is characterized by one of the greatest guitar signatures in history, and didn't do badly for Camper Van Beethoven either.

San Francisco-area bands were at the epicenter of the psychedelic scene.

Traffic: *Hole In My Shoe/Smiling Phases* (United Artists 50218, 1967): **$12**

A young Stevie Winwood catches the spirit of the time with a lyric which surely causes him pain even today—particularly as it was written by Dave Mason. Conceived at a time when the band was inaugurating what would become one of rock's better-known institutions—"getting our heads together in the country, man"—"Hole In My Shoe" has everything, from a dippy spoken word midriff, to a verse which threatened to get obscene but settled on obtuse instead.

John's Children: *Smashed Blocked/Strange Affair* (White Whale 239, 1966): **$30**

John's Children's debut single was renamed "The Love I Thought I'd Found" in the UK, for fear of its true title sending a nation's worth of kids off on an endless drug binge. But with its spoken word intro, soaring chorus, and a taste for tart sound effects, it was sonic psych before its time.

Small Faces: *Donkey Rides, A Penny A Glass/The Universal* (Immediate 5009, 1968): **$20**

There are a lot of things this song isn't. First off, it's not the Small Faces best-known song (that'd be "Itchycoo Park") nor the a-side of this 45 (that was "The Universal"). And it isn't even Steve Marriott's most archetypically psychedelic ode. Nevertheless, "Donkey Rides" so ideally captured the spirit of age that the song itself became a virtual manifesto for his immediate future.

The Crazy World of Arthur Brown: *Fire/Rest Cure* (Atlantic 2556, 1968): **$10**

An international hit, Brown's dark world of Satan, pain and purgatory had little in common with the peace and love being espoused elsewhere at the time. But the Crazy World captured a sound that is quintessential 1968—a reminder that the summer of love was indeed followed by several long seasons of cultural and political discontent.

The Yardbirds: *Happening 10 Years Time Ago /The Nazz Are Blue* (Columbia 5-10094, 1966): **$20**

Another bunch of bluesmen casting anxious eyes toward the Next Big Thing, the Yardbirds sadly went so far off the rails in their bid to jump on the psychedelic bandwagon that it's impossible to believe this is where it started. Fired by the twin assault of guitarists Jimmy Page and Jeff Beck (who supplies the hilarious "man in the street" passage during the scything instrumental break), "Happenings" was the last truly great Yardbirds single. And it was *truly* great.

The Rolling Stones: *She's a Rainbow/2,000 Light Years From Home* (London 906, 1967): **$30**

Like The Beatles, the Stones were ready for psych, having already

BILL GRAHAM PRESENTS IN SAN FRANCISCO
YARDBIRDS
LIGHTS BY THE HOLY SEE
CECIL TAYLOR
it's a Beautiful day
may 23, 24, 25
the FILLMORE
LEE CONKLIN ©1968 BILL GRAHAM
TICKETS

glanced in that insurgent direction with 1966's *Between the Buttons*. Unlike the Beatles, their efforts to embrace its ethics were less than warmly received, with *Their Satanic Majesties Request*, the album from which this single was culled, still dividing their fans down the middle. That said, this 45 sparkles in every regard, with the b-side, a paean to the vast emptiness of space, remaining one of the band's most powerful vinyl performances.

The Idle Race: *Here We Go Round the Lemon Tree/My Father's Son* (Liberty 55997): **$30**

Jeff Lynne was toying with his dreams of out-Beatle-ing The Beatles long before ELO finally gave him the opportunity to really go out of his head. The UK 45 "Skeleton and the Roundabout" is probably Idle Race's finest effort, the cautionary tale of a ghost train skeleton who ate too much (eh?), but this swirling epic likewise has much in common with Lynne's future work with both ELO and the Move.

Pretty Things: *Private Sorrow/Balloon Burning* (Rare Earth 5005, 1969): **$30**

The entire *SF Sorrow* album is generally regarded as the Pretty Thing's masterpiece, at least following their departure from the R&B that made their name, and it feels strange hearing two of its key cuts in isolation. Which may be why the single, like the band's tenure with Motown's rock label, feels somewhat ill conceived. But it's captivating, regardless.

Eric Burdon & the Animals: *When I Was Young/A Girl Called Sandoz* (MGM 13721): **$10**

What was it about beat boom bluesmen that they all had to rush into the peace and love stakes, the moment the pubs stopped serving real ale? Burdon's Animals were, however, a far more viable musical entity than history sometimes allows, faltering only when long-time listeners paused to actually listen to some of the stuff coming out of Burdon's mouth. One rhyme here deserves particular attention; "I smoked my first cigarette at 10, and for girls I had a bad yen." Indeed.

The Who: *Magic Bus/Someone's Coming* (Decca 32362, 1968): **$20**

Before "Baba O'Riley", before *Tommy*, before the Who became something to be very, very scared of, they were a top notch pop group, crashing out classic single after classic single, and this was one of them, a shifting, rattling sandstorm of echo and percussion that would grow up to become one of their greatest (and most extended) live highlights, too.

The Move: *Blackberry Way/Something* (A&M 1020, 1968): **$15**

One of the Move and, by extension, songwriter Roy Wood's greatest compositions, which in turn renders it among the finest 45s of the British 1960s, "Blackberry Way" needs no intro to set the mood; it simply declares itself with its title, then marches arm-in-glorious-arm with the Kinks' "Autumn Almanac" into the most melancholy fall you can imagine.

Donovan: *Hurdy Gurdy Man/Teen Angel* (Epic 10345, 1968): **$8**

Steve Hillage would later launch "Hurdy Gurdy Man" into spaces which Don only dreamed of, but this whirling prototype still has the same effect as a night on a very weird town, while reminding us that for all his folkie reference points, Donovan was true psych's Poet laureate.

Simon Dupree & the Big Sound: *Kites/Like the Sun, Like the Fire* (Tower 377, 1967): **$15**

Forerunners, but not forewarning, of prog monsters Gentle Giant, SD & TBS effectively restyled Traffic's "Hole In My Shoe" by exaggerating its most "wow, far out man" aspects, and then roping in a female spoken wordsmith for some mystic Eastern magic. In other words, pure psychedelia-by-numbers, but you can't help but admire their nerve.

Early in his career, not to be confused with the lead singer of the Monkees, David Jones changed his name to David Bowie.
Image courtesy Heritage Auctions

IT STARTED WITH "STARMAN"

COLLECTING DAVID BOWIE

WHEN DAVID BOWIE HIT THE UK Top Ten in the summer of 1972 with his latest single "Starman," he did more than relieve himself of the three-year-old tag of One Hit Wonder, beneath which he had labored since 1969's "Space Oddity."

He also set in motion a career that alternately enthralled, infuriated, but never stopped entertaining for the next forty-four years, until his death in January 2016. And that, in turn, ignited a collecting passion which could scarcely have been guessed at in 1972… but which was being loudly prophesied regardless.

That November, even as Bowie's follow-up "John I'm Only Dancing" slipped down the British chart, one of his former labels, Pye, released an EP of four 1960s recordings beneath the title *For the Collector: Early David Bowie*. At a time when nobody was even aware there was much of anything to collect.

It did the trick, though. I was 12 at the time, and had never imagined that owning his latest two hits and his current album in any way made me a collector.

But the EP changed my thinking altogether, at the same time as his current label, RCA, added to the excitement by reissuing two earlier albums, *Space Oddity* and *The Man Who Sold the World*; at the same time as I started to notice another LP, *The World of David Bowie*, glittering from the budget-priced bins; at the same time as I began to despair whether I'd ever be able to keep up with the flood.

Six months before, I'd scarcely heard of the man. By the time Christmas was over, I had four LPs, four singles ("Jean Genie" was released that December), and there was a new album scheduled for the following April. Another would arrive that Christmas, and *another*—a sixties anthology called *Images*—would sit temptingly in the import racks, bedecked, incidentally, in what remains the most distinctive artwork to ever have graced any David Bowie LP.

And I'd still no idea of what else was lurking out there.

Today's Bowie's pre-history is a matter of record, and a lot of records, too. In 1973-74, it was considerably less well documented. Well do I recall walking into the old Vintage Record Centre off north London's Caledonian Road, and inquiring, very casually, if they happened to have a copy of "Liza Jane" by the King Bees—a hopelessly obscure single by a hopelessly obscure band, released on a hopelessly obscure Decca subsidiary in 1964.

The guy behind the counter was not deceived. "You just read that book, didn't you?" he replied, and I had. In 1974, author George Tremlett published *The David Bowie Story,* a slender paperback that concluded with the first full discography Bowie's fans had ever seen. And there we learned that, back in 1964, Bowie cut his first record with a beat group called the King Bees.

He was David Jones in those days, soon to become Davy Jones, and make a couple of other singles, with the Manish Boys and the Lower Third.

The shop didn't have any of them, by the way. Very few stores, it has since transpired, ever did.

Jones signed to Pye and changed his name to avoid being confused with the newly-emergent Monkee; now he was David Bowie, and he cut three 45s, meaning there were still two more songs that the EP didn't cover; then moved to Decca's Deram subsidiary for a self-titled debut album full of whimsical vaudeville and chirpy ballads, a clutch of singles that sold next to nothing, and the handful of out-takes that made it onto *The World Of,* which itself was released only after he hit pay dirt with the aforementioned "Space Oddity" hit.

BILL GRAHAM PRESENTS IN SAN FRANCISCO
DAVID
BOWIE
HALLOWEEN WEEKEND
ALSO APPEARING
SYLVESTER AND HIS HOT BAND
PHLORESCENT LEECH AND EDDIE
FRI·SAT OCT 27·28TH
WINTERLAND
POST & STIENER SAN FRANCISCO
TICKETRON
$4.00 ADVANCE $4.50 AT DOOR TICKETS AVAILABLE AT ALL TICKETRON OUTLETS INCLUDING
ALL SEARS, MONTGOMERY WARD, AND EMPORIUM STORES FOR INFO CALL 692 2921

That, too, prompted an album (released in Britain, again, as *David Bowie*, in the U.S. as *Man of Words, Man of Music*, and then reissued beneath the title it should have borne all along). It failed.

More singles followed, and each of them bombed. So did *The Man Who Sold The World*; and so, upon release, did *Hunky Dory* in early 1972. Not until "Starman" and the attendant *The Rise and Fall of Ziggy Stardust and the Spiders from Mars* album finally returned him to the charts did any of those records finally break cover, and suddenly Bowie's recent past appeared to be everywhere, with more straining to break out behind it.

And the great thing is, Bowie knew how much we wanted to hear it.

Although fellow collectors will doubtless howl in disagreement, Bowie always spared a thought for the lifelong fans among his followers. He just didn't make a fuss about it.

"John I'm Only Dancing" was a non-LP 45, and when he recorded a fresh version of the same song during his *Aladdin Sane* sessions, the new take replaced the old one on repressings of the existing single without a word to anyone. Another of that album's out-takes, reworking one of the doomed singles from 1970, "Holy Holy," turned up on a b-side a year or so later.

A *Ziggy* out-take, a cover of Chuck Berry's "Round and Round," made it out on another b-side; "Amsterdam," a Jacques Brel song of similar vintage, was released on yet another.

He scored a massive hit with "Rebel Rebel," then snuck a completely new arrangement of it onto an American promo single. No fuss, no warning, no mile high headlines proclaiming what he'd done. He just pulled the songs out of the archive, and let the collectors work out what they were.

Tamsin Darke, author of the authoritative *Rare Records Price Guide* to Bowie's UK and U.S. singles, explains, "throughout his career, David constantly took flak from fans who accused him of not giving them 'the rare stuff,' when what they really meant was, he wasn't giving them *enough* rare stuff.

"It really was a case of 'damned if you, damned if you don't'; he put out two *Aladdin Sane* out-takes, the fans wanted two more. He released a host of out-takes and rarities when his albums were given the bonus treatment by Rykodisc in 1990, the first major artist to do so; the fans moaned because he didn't put out two hosts. And so on."

So on indeed. The early 1980s brought an official release for the 1973 concert at which he retired Ziggy Stardust; while the 21st century saw concerts dating as far back as 1970 make it out aboard releases that were targeted almost wholly at collectors.

"Bowie's problem, if you can call it that, is he was just so prolific," continues Darke. "Forget about how many albums he released, he was always talking about ones that he hadn't released, or that he was planning. So they were added to the collector's catalog of 'unreleased' material, when in some cases he might not actually have written a single song… it was just a planned album, after all."

Indeed, it is worth noting that when, in 2000, Bowie *did* record what he intended to be his next album, only for his then-record label to turn it down, he made certain that almost every song intended for the record subsequently made it out on either a b-side or a compilation. And the fact that the majority of those songs were brand new remakes of records he'd made back in the 1960s proves that he remained as conscious of his past achievements as the most devoted Bowie collector.

To focus upon what Bowie did or didn't permit to escape the archive, however, is to overlook the records that he did release, and which established him among rock's most avidly collected artists in the first place.

Once out of the 1960s, few are truly rare. Among his earliest singles, however, there are some eye-watering prices: Darke's book (published shortly after Bowie's death) values the King Bees' UK debut at $5,000; and its two immediate successors at $1,500, the same price accorded to Bowie's debut American single, 1966's "Can't Help Thinking About Me" (Warner Bros. 5815).

Thereafter, even the high prices tend to stay within the realm of low three figures, with only the occasional leap into what we might call the stratosphere; a rare British picture sleeve version of "Space Oddity" (issued at a time when few UK singles boasted such adornments) is valued at $3,500; a withdrawn American release for "Janine" at $4,000. And by 1972, when Bowie signed with RCA, it is again picture sleeves that boost the majority of releases beyond even $20 or so.

That said, Darke does offer up a fascinating table of worldwide rarities, which we reproduce here with her kind permission.

The Prettiest Star (Japan—promo 45) —**$8,000** (sold 2015)

Love You Till Tuesday (South Africa Deram 1967)—**$7,393** (sold 2013)

Memory of a Free Festival (Scandinavia pic sleeve)—**$6,947** (sold 2013)

Rebel Rebel (Mexico EP)—**$6,889** (sold 2014)

Sorrow (Mexico promo 45)—**$6,100** (sold 2013)

The Prettiest Star (Italy—picture sleeve)—**$5,865** (sold 2013)

Let's Spend the Night Together (India pic sleeve)—**$3,999** (sold 2012)

The Laughing Gnome (Belgium demo 1967) —**$3,697** (sold 2011)

The rarest of the rare, however, comes from somewhat closer to home. In 1973, RCA in the U.S. released a single of "Time," a track from his latest album, *Aladdin Sane* (again) and popped it into a picture sleeve that mirrored the parent attraction.

And then they popped it out again. Nobody knows why. But "Time" went on sale with no picture sleeve at all… except for the handful, if that, of copies which had one.

From all accounts, the sleeve remained almost completely unknown until 1998, when a photograph appeared in *Goldmine's 45 RPM Picture Sleeve Price Guide.*

A full decade later, a copy of the sleeve appeared at auction for the first time. The cover was slightly scratched and the record was slightly warped, but still it was bid up to $3,550—a sum that more than doubled when a Near Mint copy was listed on eBay in 2013. Valued today at $8,000, "Time" has been described, and perhaps rightfully so, as the rarest of all U.S. picture sleeves.

But it is not Bowie's only highly priced sleeve. Alluded to already in these pages, the first pressings of his 1974 *Diamond Dogs* album featured a portrait by Belgian artist Guy Peellaert, depicting Bowie with a long canine body—whose legs were parted just enough to permit a glimpse of the animal's genitals.

Faster than you can say "butcher cover," RCA withdrew the sleeve, airbrushed away the offending view, and the album release went ahead as planned, its naughty elements hidden from view until 2016 restored the original design within Bowie's *Who Can I Be Now 1974-1976* box set.

Inevitably, however, a handful of copies escaped the purge, to assure Bowie's place in any listing of America's rarest LPs.

Like the "Time" sleeve, however, this edition of *Diamond Dogs* is an anomaly within the overall context of Bowie's cataloged career. The bulk of

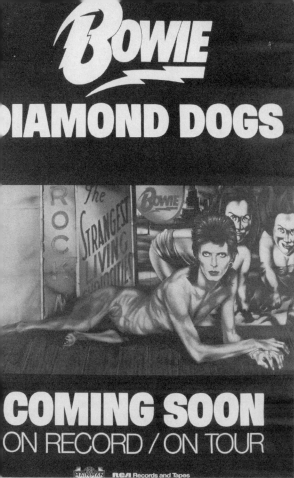

his releases—27 studio albums, nine live albums, and over 100 singles—all remain readily obtainable in something approaching their initial release, as well as within a variety of limited edition special packages.

Some were bundled together in a series of newly picture-sleeved singles; others were repressed as picture discs. Indeed, as of this writing, we are six years into a fresh series of picture disc singles, each one released to celebrate the fortieth anniversary of its original release, and some of these have already sky-rocketed in price.

We are also two volumes into a series of chronological box set vinyl reissues (the aforementioned *Who Can I Be Now, 1974-1976* and *Five Years 1969-1973*); and as your collection grows, you realize (if you had not comprehended it beforehand) just how remarkably versatile, not to mention unconventional, Bowie's vision of a mainstream rock career really was.

Who else would have recorded a Christmas single with Bing Crosby

(1982's "Peace On Earth"/"Little Drummer Boy" medley)…

… would have narrated *Peter and the Wolf* on an album for his son (1978's *Peter and the Wolf*)… released an album of sixties cover versions just as the world acclaimed him one of rock's greatest songwriters (1973's *Pin Ups*)… taped a soundtrack for his movie debut that has still not been heard in its entirety (1975's *The Man Who Fell to Earth*)… and delivered an album comprising two minute vignettes on one side, and vast instrumental caverns on the other, and then effectively gave it to his label for nothing, because that's the only way he could persuade them to release it. And they *still* needed a lot of persuading (1977's *Low*).

Who else would have reinvented himself as a Philly soul singer and rearranged one of his greatest rock hits as an eight-minute disco work-out ("John I'm Only Dancing"—recorded in 1975, released in 1979)?

Who else would ended the seventies by rerecording his first ever hit for a b-side (1979's "Space Oddity" remake), then opened the eighties by reprising that song's protagonist, Major Tom, and telling the world he's a junkie (1980's "Ashes to Ashes")?

Who else has recorded with Iggy Pop, Tina Turner, Lou Reed, Freddie Mercury, Mick Jagger, Brian Eno, Niles Rodgers and Mickey Rourke?

And who else stage-managed their own departure from this life with such exquisite grace and consummate style? Bowie passed away on Jan. 10, 2016, just three days after the release of his latest album, the portent-and-prophecy packed *Blackstar*, which won five Grammy Awards. "Look at me, I'm up in heaven," he sang on the record and, by the time many people heard the album for the first time, he was.

Collecting David Bowie might *sound* easy, and an evening scouring your favorite Internet outlets might even make it look easy as well. With an eye for a bargain and a couple of hundred bucks, you could have half the collection on its way to you by morning.

But collecting isn't *only* about the hunt (even though we say elsewhere that that's a major part of it). It's also about the listening, and the comprehending, too. A well-curated David Bowie collection will keep you intrigued forever.

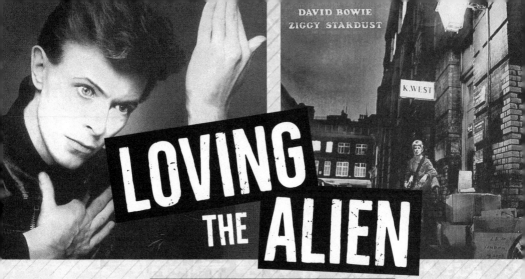

LOVING THE ALIEN

DAVID BOWIE 1967-1980

ORIGINAL ALBUM PRICE GUIDE

David Bowie (Deram DE16003, 1967)
current value: **$600**

Man of Words, Man of Music
(Mercury SR61246, 1969): **$700**

The Man Who Sold the World
(Mercury SR61325, 1970): **$100**

Hunky Dory
(RCA Victor LSP-4623, 1972): **$65**

**The Rise and Fall of Ziggy Stardust
and the Spiders from Mars**
(RCA Victor LSP-4702, 1972): **$75**

Aladdin Sane (RCA Victor LSP-4852,
1973): **$75**

Images 1966-1967
(London PS628/9, 1973): **$60**

Pin Ups
(RCA Victor APL1-0291, 1973): **$60**

Diamond Dogs (RCA Victor CPL1-0576,
1974—withdrawn sleeve): **$5,000**

Diamond Dogs
(RCA Victor CPL1-0576, 1974): **$40**

David Live
(RCA Victor CPL2-0771, 1974): **$60**

Young Americans
(RCA Victor APL1-0998, 1975): **$50**

Station to Station
(RCA Victor APL1-1327, 1976): **$50**

Changesonebowie
(RCA Victor APL1-1732, 1976): **$40**

Low (RCA Victor APL1-2030, 1977): **$50**

Starting Point
(London LC50007, 1977): **$15**

Heroes (RCA Victor AFL1-2522, 1977): **$50**

Stage (RCA Victor CPL2-2913, 1978): **$40**

Peter and the Wolf
(RCA Red Seal ARL1-2743, 1978): **$50**

Bowie Now (RCA Victor DJL1-2697,
1978): **$175**

Lodger (RCA Victor AYL1-4234, 1981): **$25**

Scary Monsters (& Super Creeps)
(RCA Victor AQL1-3647, 1980): **$50**

Scary Monsters Interview
(RCA Victor DJL1-3840, 1980): **$125**

1980 All Clear
(RCA Victor DJL1-3545, 1980): **$150**

An Evening with David Bowie
(RCA Victor -, 1978): **$150**

PARAMOUNT PICTURES PRESENTS A ROBERT STIGWOOD PRODUCTION
JOHN TRAVOLTA KAREN GORNEY "SATURDAY NIGHT FEVER"
Screenplay by NORMAN WEXLER Directed by JOHN BADHAM
xecutive Producer KEVIN McCORMICK Produced by ROBERT STIGWOO
inal music written and performed by the Bee Gees Soundtrack album available on RSO Records Read the Bantam Paper

CHAPTER 17

DANCING AT THE DISCO BALL

AUTHOR AMY HANSON IS RESOLUTE. "Although Disco is now synonymous with mirror balls, polyester and Tony Manero, it really brought together much, much, more. Disco was not just a cheesy music spectacular; it was a cultural lifestyle drawn from a subcultural milieu which might have started small, but would, by the time it was done eating the country, ultimately expand into almost every household in the United States."

Discussing the disco phenomenon in *Goldmine* magazine in October 1997, Hanson wrote "Disco is defined musically within fairly rigid guidelines. It brings together a thumping beat with strings, horns and plastic sexuality.

"Musically, it was totally genuine; even the grand orchestral arrangements were real. There were few synthesizers at the time capable of providing the lush and sweeping body assault of an orchestra of violins. Same with horns.

"One can only imagine how classical string quartets suffered during the Disco revolution, as their members were plucked to become slaves to session rooms in studios all across the country."

As sorely, perhaps, as the rock artists, past and present, who themselves

1977's megahit *Saturday Night Fever* catapulted disco into the mainstream and the Bee Gees into stardom. And, despite the white leisure suit, It wasn't too bad for John Travolta's career either.
Image courtesy Heritage Auctions

leaped aboard the disco bandwagon to breathe new, or at least extra-marketable life into their careers.

The Rolling Stones ("Miss You"), Kiss ("I Was Made For Loving You"), Paul McCartney ("Goodnight Tonight") and, most notoriously of all, Rod Stewart ("Do Ya Think I'm Sexy") all rode the disco beat to a new sphere of success, while vintage soul and R&B acts by the barrel-load sidestepped what the critics called the "purity" of their earlier recordings, to introduce their muse to a brand new audience.

Disco was birthed in the US in the early-mid 1970s, emerging—of course—out of the discotheques that had long been a staple of the club scene.

New York journalist Vince Aletti began tracking the new, and hottest dance songs as early as 1973 in a *Rolling Stone* article; and, by the following November, he was penning a weekly column of reviews and charts for *Record World* magazine.

Indeed, reading through the book that compiles those columns, the very sensibly titled *The Disco Files 1973-1978* (published by DJHistory. com), one can still sense the excitement as it inexorably built up—from the earliest columns, when Aletti was still spotlighting European imports and unreleased acetates; through the release of Gloria Gaynor's *Never Can Say Goodbye* LP, with its mold-breaking sequencing of its full side one into one seamless non-stop dance party; and into the golden age post-*Saturday Night Fever,* when every disco hit was a pop chart smash as well.

Slowly, as Hanson put it, "the cumulative effect of records like George McCrae's 'Rock Your Baby,' Jim Gilstrap's 'Swing Your Daddy,' Carl Douglas' 'Kung Fu Fighting,' a host of early Harry 'KC' Casey's Sunshine Band hits, and the novelty hits by Disco Tex… did the trick.

"The term Disco was already in wide, and none-too-discriminating use long before the genre itself was formularized. By the time Labelle threw 'Lady Marmalade' into the brew, in 1974, the die was already cast. And by 1976, that same song's basic recipe of rhythm, beat, strings and sex was being liberally spread across American radio, and by some of radio's best-loved stalwarts."

Disco's first dedicated collectors were, hardly surprisingly, the disc jockeys who first introduced the music to the dance floor, and whose audience was singlehandedly responsible for deciding whether or not a record broke big.

For the first time in the modern musical era, radio had absolutely nothing to do with a record, or an artist's success. It was the dance floors that dictated who was destined for greater things, and who was consigned to the dumpster… at least until they brought out a new record.

Few people who heard it for the first time in a disco will ever forget

Donna Summer's orgasmic hit "Love to Love You Baby" was banned on some radio stations as too suggestive.

their introduction to Donna Summer's "Love to Love You Baby," another side-long suite, comprised almost wholly of seductive strings and orgasmic moaning. As a three minute single, it was effective enough. But as a 17- minute symphony, it sent the birthrate soaring.

That was in 1975; two years later, the discos sent another Summer single soaring, only this time it was the electronic motorik of "I Feel Love," a record that has subsequently been credited with birthing everything from electronic rock to synthipop, and remains among the most influential records ever released.

The dance floors determined hits, and they perpetuated them too. When Van McCoy coined a rhythm called "The Hustle," audiences swiftly developed the moves to match it, and another cultural leviathan was born, a craze for the *dance du jour*, which Hanson describes as "unparalleled since the early Sixties."

Diana Ross's "Love Hangover" in early 1976 was another pivotal moment. Seven minutes long, with Ross at her super-softest, super- sexiest, and a bass line that left listeners powerless to resist, "Love Hangover" confirmed disco's ascendancy at the same time as it let the record companies know that there was a market now for a medium that had hitherto scarcely registered in the marketplace—the twelve-inch single.

"Love Hangover" was only ever made commercially available as a full-length LP track, and a harshly edited 45. A 12-inch single, dedicated to the album version, was produced but it was intended only for DJs—of whom there was an ever-growing tribe, far more than the number of copies available.

Public demand for a copy of the 12-inch went unheeded, and the modern value of the DJ disc today reflects both its continued scarcity and the lingering demand. Had "Love Hangover" been released to the public in this form, it might have been Motown's biggest record ever. It wasn't

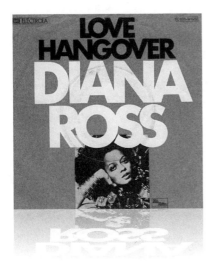

(although it still did well), but neither Motown nor any other label with a disco dream was going to make the same mistake again.

In fact Motown was very much caught on the hop by disco. The late Frankie Gaye, whose brother Marvin later hit similar heights with "Got To Give It Up," recalled, "Motown had led the black music world for so long that when disco came along, they naturally assumed that they would be able to lead that as well. But the label's strengths simply didn't go in that direction. There was an element in disco, or maybe missing from it, which Motown simply couldn't come to terms with."

Yvonne Fair's "It Shoulda Been Me," Marvin Gaye's "Got To Give It Up," and the Commodores' slow dance classics "Easy" and "Three Times A Lady" aside, Motown's only other major contribution to disco was Thelma Houston's "Don't Leave Me This Way," and for that they had to turn to one of their own greatest rivals, Philadelphia-based Kenny Gamble and Leon Huff's Philly International.

That label's own dominance of the dance floors and, subsequently, the collectors market, is indistinguishable from the history of disco.

So many of the genre's greatest hits stemmed from the Philly International stable, with the likes of the O'Jays, Billy Paul, MFSB and, best of all, Harold Levin and the Bluenotes contributing some of disco's most deathless moments—indeed, if Houston's "Don't Leave Me This Way" can be ranked among the greatest disco records ever made, Melvin's own original performance of the same song runs it a very close second.

It was with the advent of the 12-inch single, gradually throughout 1976 and 1977, before the floodgates opened for the end of the decade, that disco collecting could truly be said to have begun—in as much as fans were no longer forced to scramble through the used bins searching for any discs a DJ might have disposed of; or, even more challenging, trying to convince one to sell off a favorite record for less than an arm and a leg.

In Europe, Boney M, the vocals-only brainchild of German producer Frank Farian were among the first to take advantage of the format, with a string of 12-inch singles that soared up the UK chart; in the U.S., their debut

"Daddy Cool" appeared only as a promo and routinely sells for around $30 today.

Barry White, a veteran producer and songwriter who had been creating vast slow dance orchestrations for several highly successful years, was another pioneer—his Love Unlimited Orchestra's "Theme from King Kong" was released in 1976, and is likewise much sought after.

But the new format's appeal was obvious to all. Whether spinning at 33 or 45 (different US labels made different decisions, although European releases are routinely 45), the expanded vinyl surface allowed far more music to be packed on, usually in the form of "extended mixes" that could be anything from a few repeats of the regular three minutes, with maybe a repetitive drum break dropped into the middle, to whole new performances of the song.

Another Boney M masterpiece, "Rasputin," had already proved a disco smash in its album format, as it pulsed out of the title track to *Night Flight to Venus*. Released as a single, Farian then extended "Rasputin" to over seven minutes, allowing quick witted disc jockeys to create their own seamless segues and keep the rhythm pounding for a quarter of an hour.

There were times when it was difficult to even distinguish between an album and a 12-inch. Indeed, in the U.S., Cerrone's "Love in C Minor" was released as a side-long 16-minute LP track, with only two further songs on the b-side; in the Netherlands, the precise same configuration was marketed as a 12-inch. (In the UK, however, when a 12-inch was called for, the label bizarrely deployed the edited three-minute version!)

However these vast new expanses of vinyl were used, the 12-inch was the enterprising disco artist's playground, in the same way as 45s propelled the British Invasion, and albums sustained psychedelia.

Disco LPs were being made, of course, and depending upon the minds behind the music (which a lot of times meant the producer, as opposed to the performer), some magnificent statements were made.

Possibly inspiring what would soon become a mania for disco-fying classic oldies ("Knock On Wood," "Nights in White Satin," "Don't Let Me Be Misunderstood"… the list was endless), another German producer, Jurgen Korduletschm was responsible for *At The Discotheque*, credited to Lipstique and offering up deranged covers of "Venus," "Light My Fire" and, most peculiarly of all, "Mah Na Mah Na," stripped of all comic overtones and delivered instead as a string driven sex machine.

Other albums had other virtues. But still the 12-inch single remained disco's natural home, and some magnificent music made it out beneath its auspices: Sylvester's "You Make Me Feel (Mighty Real)," Anita Ward's "Ring My Bell," Gloria Gaynor's "I Will Survive," A Taste of Honey's "Boogie Oogie Oogie," Candi Staton's "Young Hearts Run Free," Alicia Bridges' "I Love

ONE HUNDRED AND FORTY-FOUR INCHES OF DISCO HEAVEN

Diana Ross: *Love Hangover* (7:49)/I Want You (Vocal 4:33) (Instrumental 4:36) (Motown PR-16, 1976): **$200**

Bee Gees: *You Should Be Dancing* (B-side blank) (RSO RS853, 1976): **$150**

Funkadelic: *One Nation Under a Groove* (11:26) (Instrumental 5:26)(Warner Bros. PRO-A-766, 1978): **$150**

Rose Royce: *Do Your Dance* (9:15)/Wishing on a Star (4:50)/It Makes You Feel Like Dancin' (8:43)/ Ooh Boy (4:15)(Whitfield PRO695, 1977): **$150**

Cerrone: *Love in C Minor/ Cerrone's Paradise* (Atlantic DK4623, 1978): **$100**

Deniece Williams: *Free/It's Important to Me* (Columbia 23-10513, 1977): **$100**

A Taste of Honey: *Boogie Oogie Oogie* (5:37)/Disco Dancin' (5:53)(Capitol 8507, 1978): **$65**

Lipps Inc.: *Funkytown* (7:51)/ (B-side blank)(Casablanca NBD-20207, 1980): **$65**

Peaches and Herb: *Shake Your Groove Thing* (6:36) (same on both sides) (Polydor PRO 055, 1978) current value: **$65**

Chic: *Le Freak* (5:30)/Savoir Faire (5:02) (Atlantic DSK0131, 1978): **$50**

Crown Heights Affair: *Do It the French Way/Sexy Ways* (De-Lite DDS582, 1977): **$50**

Sister Sledge: *He's the Greatest Dancer* (6:04)/We Are Family (8:06) (Cotillion DSK0144, 1979): **$40**

the Night Life," McFadden and Whitehead's "Ain't No Stopping Us Now,"
Cerrone's "Supernature," Lipps Inc's "Funkytown," Musique's "In the Bush,"
Andrea True Connection's "More More More."… And, indeed, more, more,
more.

In fact the only thing that disco couldn't do was launch more than a
handful of lasting careers. There was the Bee Gees, of course, courtesy of
their starring musical role in the *Saturday Night Fever* phenomenon, but
they'd been stars for a decade already, and disco was just one more halt on
their musical journey.

Donna Summer, too, survived the era, but far, far more of the familiar
disco names are best remembered today as the answers to a "one-hit
wonder" trivia quiz.

One single, maybe a couple, and that was all they could hope for, and
might even be all that some of them expected. In terms of actual record
production, disco had less in common with the likes of Motown and Philly
International than it did with the first years of rock 'n' roll, when hungry
entrepreneurs would haul good-looking kids out of the audience and
promise to make them a star. A couple of singles and a photo-op later, the

kids were back on the street and the shark would be cruising off in search of the next pretty face.

But the records they made, for as long as they lasted (and disco was effectively finished by the dawn of the eighties), not only remain immortal, they also remain familiar, blasting out of oldies radio and staples of Remember the Seventies style collections.

The seven-inch versions, which we most commonly encounter in those arenas, however, are but insignificant fragments on the art that was woven across the 12-inch mix, in the same way that the famous bit of Beethoven's Fifth Symphony really is merely that, the famous bit.

To appreciate the music, you need to hear it in its entirety, and nowhere else in record collecting can that be said to be truer than at the disco.

The disco 12-inch collection awaits you. And you don't even have to dance to it. Unless you want to.

CHAPTER 18

PUB AND PUNK ROCK

A SAFETY PIN STUCK IN MY HEART

IT IS OLD NEWS NOW, that the advent of Internet shopping opened a vast array of new worlds to record collectors, not merely allowing the market-place to embrace hoards of records that had hitherto sat untouched in attics, but allowing stores and sellers all over the world to reach out to a likewise worldwide customer base.

Today, collectors who previously considered their hobby restricted to domestic releases alone are able to branch out in all directions—Japanese pressings, once considered (by virtue of their generally superior pressing quality) the gold standard of collectibles, and priced accordingly, can be purchased direct from source; while the wide availability of European releases has opened collections up to the deepest secrets of those countries' music scenes. And so on.

The greatest boon for many collectors, however, has been the availability of UK releases—not only the original versions of those British Invasion era albums that the American labels sliced and diced into oft-times unrecognizable collections, but also the vast quantity of records that never saw a domestic release, but whose reputation preceded them nonetheless.

This is especially true of what history now refers to as the punk era,

Never Mind the Bollocks, Here's the Sex Pistols, 1977 promo poster for the Sex Pistols.
Image courtesy Heritage Auctions

that short span at the end of the 1970s when bands like the Sex Pistols, the Damned, the Clash and the Jam amassed UK discographies that utterly dwarf their U.S. counterparts, while other headline groups—the Adverts, the Ruts and Johnny Moped among them—did not even have U.S. record deals.

They were available on import, of course, but they were often costly and, besides, entered the country in such comparatively limited quantities that they remained rare for decades thereafter. Now, many of them can be picked up for what often feel like bargain prices.

Among collectors of punk and its various offspring, two record labels in particular continue to utterly bedazzle.

Stiff and Chiswick were both London-based operations, founded in the mid-1970s, before "punk" was even a twinkle in the eye, but regarded now in the eyes of rock historians as midwives to the entire phenomenon.

The aforementioned Adverts and Johnny Moped both launched

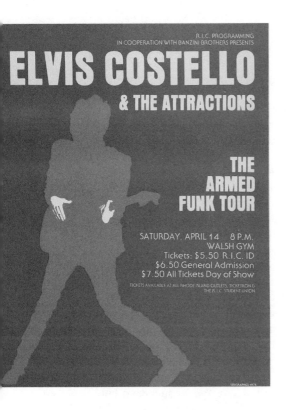

R.I.C. PROGRAMMING
IN COOPERATION WITH BANZINI BROTHERS PRESENTS

ELVIS COSTELLO
& THE ATTRACTIONS

**THE
ARMED
FUNK TOUR**

SATURDAY, APRIL 14   8 P.M.
WALSH GYM
Tickets: $5.50 R.I.C. ID
$6.50 General Admission
$7.50 All Tickets Day of Show

TICKETS AVAILABLE AT ALL RHODE ISLAND OUTLETS, TICKETRON &
THE R.I.C. STUDENT UNION

their careers on one or the other label; so did the Damned (Stiff), the Rings (Chiswick) and Motorhead (both!); and many more besides. And if one delves deeper into the two label's catalogs, particularly throughout their earlier releases, one will find evidence of a musical force that scarcely even registered in this country, but whose impact was still being felt here into the early eighties.

Pub rock was the university from which many of punk and the new wave's later heroes graduated. Nick Lowe, Elvis Costello, Ian Gomm, Graham Parker and the Rumour, 999, Ian Dury and the Blockheads, the Clash's Joe Strummer and many, many more all cut their performing teeth on the pub rock circuit—which was exactly what it sounds like; a circuit of venues, for the most part pubs and bars, around which a small army of bands paraded, far from the spotlight of media, often ignored by the major record labels, content simply to play exactly what they wanted to the people who wanted to hear from it.

Occasionally one would break out into the "big time"—in late 1976, the R&B band Dr. Feelgood scored a UK number one hit with their live album *Stupidity*. But they were the exception that proved the rule. Not until Punk became the leading fashion and style of the day did the pub rock brigade truly begin reaping the rewards they had deserved for so long.

The important thing to remember is that there was never a single pub rock sound or an easy way to define a pub rock band. Anything from Americanized country to fifties-style rock 'n' roll; from ferocious funk to what Graham Parker called angry Motown; could be, and was, accommodated beneath the pub rock banner, a broad school that contains, even today, some of the most exciting music ever recorded.

The following rounds up twenty-five of the scene's most powerful practitioners.

The Flying Aces: *Welcome to the Party* (from the UK various artists LP Christmas at the Patti; United Artists UDX 205/6, 1973): **$80**

Christmas At The Patti itself was a double-ten-inch live album headlined by Man, but overflowing with friends and relatives—this was Martin (ex-Mighty Baby) and Georgina Ace's vibrant set opener.

Dr. Feelgood: *Roxette* (from the UK album Down By The Jetty; United Artists UAS 29727, 1975): **$30**

First sighted outside London when they opened for Dave Edmunds and Brinsley Schwarz on the 1974 New Favourites tour, for many people, the Feelgoods *were* pub rock. Tight, staccato R&B, growling vocals, machine gun etiquette, the Feelgoods dressed like gangsters, played like Pirates, and their first single, like their debut album, was turned down for release in the U.S. because they recorded the whole thing in mono!

Kokomo: *I Can Understand It* (from the album Kokomo; Columbia PC 33442, 1975): **$18**

Sharing the stage with the Feelgoods and Chilli Willi, Kokomo were one of the attractions of the Naughty Rhythms tour (January-February 1975), even as they recorded a self-titled album, which the British press would describe as one of the best of the decade so far, and which also earned a rare pub rock release in America.

It was a strange gig for a former King Crimson horn player (Mel Collins), plus ex-members of Vinegar Joe, Arrival and the Chris Stainton Band, but weirder things still were to happen. Rightly feted as the best British funk band since the Average White Band, you know those horns on Dylan's *Desire* album? That was Kokomo.

Brinsley Schwarz: *(What's So Funny 'Bout) Peace, Love & Understanding* (from the UK album New Favourites Of Brinsley Schwarz; United Artists UAS 29641, 1974): **$25**

After having four albums released in the U.S. through Capitol, the Brinsleys were dropped and promptly delivered a fifth, which led off with what became their best loved, and most successful song ever—albeit in the later hands of Elvis Costello.

Ducks Deluxe: *Please Please Please* (from the album Ducks Deluxe; RCA LPL1-5008, 1973): **$18**

Another rare pub rock import that did not need to be bought from the import stores, Ducks Deluxe's greatest downfall was that their records never captured the sheer magnificence of their onstage demeanor. But this is one of the songs that came close.

Bees Make Honey: *Music Every Night*
(from the UK album Music Every Night; EMI EMC 3013, 1973): **$40**

Like the ex-pat Americans of Eggs Over Easy (whom the Bees followed into a prestigious residency at the Tally Ho! pub in Kentish Town), Dublin's Bees spent their career on a distinctly country edge of the scene. But the ubiquitous "Music Every Night" summed up the scene regardless.

Graham Parker and the Rumour: *Hey Lord, Don't Ask Me Questions*
(from the album Howlin' Wind; Mercury SRM-1-1095, 1976): **$10**

Parker never understood, and rarely tolerated, his band's inclusion in the pub rock field… although the presence of several ex-Brinsley Schwarz members might have had something to do with it. Praised profusely by Bob Dylan, this song, like the album from which it is taken, illustrates both sides of the argument.

Ace: *How Long* (from the album Five-a-Side; Anchor 8308-2001 H, 1975): **$25**

Pub rock's first bona fide superstars, at least in as much as they scored a major hit on both sides of the Atlantic, Paul Carrack's Ace were never to follow up their initial success, a brooding, moody bass driven ballad which sounded great on the radio, but was even better live, where it turned into a veritable behemoth. How Long? Ooh, ten minutes or so.

The 101'ers: *Keys To Your Heart/5 Star Rock 'n' Roll Petrol*
(UK single; Chiswick S3, 1976): **$20**

Always worth more than the posthumous applause they received for birthing Joe Strummer, the 101'ers were also prone to coming up with some godawful song titles... as the b-side to their one and only single proves.

The Hammersmith Gorillas: *You Really Got Me/Leaving 'Ome*
(UK single; Penny Farthing PEN 849, 1974): **$25**

Years before Supergrass made distended sideburns chic, Jesse Hector and his west London Gorillas were donning baggy checkered trousers and refusing to shave properly. This rough and ready romp through the Kinks' first hit packs a fiery aggression, which even survived into punk years; so, with the bisection of their name, did the band.

Motorhead: *White Line Fever/Leaving Here* (French single; Skydog MH 001, 1977): **$80**

Long before they were absorbed by the heavy-metal brigade, Motorhead were effectively a very loud anomaly, torturing London club goers and getting thrown out of every genre they approached. Pub rock was no exception, but if we can include Kokomo.... Taken from a projected debut album, which would not see the light of day for three more years, this single was also scheduled for UK release by Stiff, only to be cancelled until the label's first compilation, *A Bunch of Stiff Records*. And talking of which….

Dave Edmunds: *Jo Jo Gunne* (from the UK various artists album A Bunch of Stiff Records; Stiff SEEZ 1, 1977): **$10**

Though Welshman Edmunds has moved through so many musical pastures that it is positively evil to nail him into one, he was very much the titular head of pub rock through the early-mid 1970s, as an influence, as a producer (aborted sessions for Motorhead, and a residency at the in-favor Rockfield Studios), and as an example of how you can spend your entire life on the road and still make cracking records.

Help Yourself: *Calapso* (from the album Beware the Shadow; United Artists UA-LA079-F, 1973): **$20**

Strumming guitars and random mock-Hispanics abound as the criminally underrated Help Yourself boogie briefly through one of the multitude of live showstoppers which record company apathy on both sides of the ocean managed to keep so well hidden.

Jess Roden Band: *Can't Get Next To You*
(from the UK EP Live!; Island IEP 3, 1976): **$10**

From the live EP, which debuted ex-Butts Band frontman Roden's latest group, seven minutes of bluesy understatement wrap up side one with unparalleled passion.

The Tyla Gang: *Styrofoam/Texas Chainsaw Massacre Boogie* (UK single Stiff Records BUY 4, 1976): **$10**

Ducks Deluxe frontman Sean Tyla returns, this time fronting his own aggregation, and the saga of a woman whose house, dog, furniture, and pretty much everything else, are made of styrofoam. What else?

Kilburn and the High Roads: *Crippled With Nerves*
(from the UK album Handsome; Dawn DNLS 3065, 1975): **$40**

Frontman Ian Dury once said he never did understand the Kilburns' failure to break through; Graham Parker reckons he never understood Dury's bemusement. You decide: from early 1975, this was also the band's sophomore single, and much of Dury's future self was already on display.

Chilli Willi and the Red Hot Peppers: *Drunken Sunken Red Neck Blues*
(from the UK album Kings Of The Robot Rhythm; Revelation REV 002, 1972): **$80**

Though relegated to the b-side of the Chilli's "Friday Song" single, this is actually a more representative airing for the band's manifold talents... talents, sadly, which were snuffed out when the band broke up immediately following the Naughty Rhythms tour ended.

The Kursaal Flyers: *Little Does She Know*
(from the UK album Golden Mile; CBS S 81622, 1976): **$10**

Thoroughly overshadowed by guitarist Will Birch's next birth in the Records, the Kursaals emerged from Southend, a seaside town in the shadow of the Feelgoods' industrial Canvey Island stomping ground. The difference in upbringing was immediately apparent; the Kursaals, named for a local funfair, had a lighthearted bent which was both instantly attractive and horribly affected; the band's sole hit single (from late 1976), captures both aspects of the band in equal quantities.

Eddie and the Hot Rods: *Gloria/Get Out of Denver* (from the UK EP Live At The Marquee; Island Records, IEP 2, 1976): **$15**

The one, the only... compared to the Rods, the rest of the pub scene were grizzled old men, both chronologically and in terms of sheer, hard-driving energy.

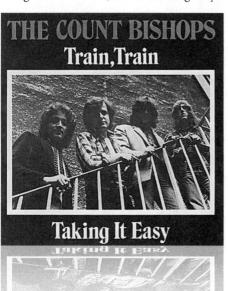

Had they emerged a mere six months later, the Rods could have ushered in punk as effectively as anyone; as it was, the new music did not phase them in the slightest, and over the course of two great albums, a clutch of singles, and the live EP from which this is culled, Southend's *other* claim to fame could transform the coldest day into a sweat bath. Magic.

The Count Bishops: *Train Train/ Taking It Easy*
(UK single; Chiswick S2, 1976): **$15**

More primal roots rock, this time from a band who looked and played like a motorcycle gang. Dirty R&B, with the emphasis on dirt, the Count Bishops debuted the Chiswick label in November 1975, with the scorching *Speedball* EP, then followed through with an even more visceral single. Previously known as Chrome, but with New Yorker Johnny Guitar joining fellow colonial Mike Spenser in the band, the Bishops are best remembered today for Spenser's role in the Sex Pistols' history (he almost got Johnny Rotten's job, before Johnny Rotten appeared); "Train Train" proves what rotten memories people have.

Nick Lowe: *Keep It Out of Sight/ Truth Drug* (Dutch single; Dynamite DYR 45007, 1976): **$25)**

Immediately post-Brinsleys, a solo Lowe takes the Dr. Feelgood growler and slows it to sinister proportions, a slinky, twitchy demon of a disc that has never appeared on any of his albums, but would have more-than-graced almost all of them.

Little Bob Story: *I'm Crying* (from the UK EP Little Bob Story; Chiswick Sw7, 1976): **$20**

In 1976, Robert Piazza's extraordinarily hairy R&B band headlined what was generally described as "the first European Punk Rock Festival" in Mont De Marsen, France. Also on the bill were the Gorillas, Nick Lowe, the Tyla Gang, Roogalator, the Hot Rods… oh, and the Damned. One out of seven ain't bad.Neither was Little Bob Story. Once described as the most credible band ever to emerge out of darkest France, albeit one prone to recording mud-caked covers of 60s classics, LBS signed to Chiswick, and the rest, as they say, *should* have been history.

Roogalator: *Cincinnati Fatback/All Aboard* (UK single; Stiff BUY 3, 1976): **$15**

They looked like geeks, and their Stiff Records debut didn't disguise the fact, even dressing the band up in *With The Beatles* album art. Inside the covers, though, Cincinnati native Danny Adler presented a very different picture, a blazing funk hybrid which conjured up nothing so much as a hungry Canned Heat, boogying on down for a pint and a pack of cigarettes.

Plummet Airlines: *Silver Shirt/This Is The World*
(UK single; Stiff BUY 8, 1976): **$15**

By late 1976, Pub Rock was clearly bracing itself for something new. The Damned had already emerged three singles earlier on Stiff; Elvis Costello was waiting in the wings. Graham Parker was among the names regarded as being capable of leading this unnamed New Wave; and so were the Feelgoods and Hot Rods. But it was Plummet Airlines who really knew what was going on: "the light is fading," they sang; "goodbye rock 'n' roll."

Supercharge: *She Moved The Dishes First*
(from the UK album Local Lads Make Good; Virgin V 2053, 1976): **$15**

But we cannot end on such a portentous note, especially when one of the greatest of all Pub bands remains unmentioned. Supercharge, led by the chrome domed magnificence of saxman Albie Donnelly, were more or less a scaled down funk band, famed for a 1976 single called "Get Down Boogie"... principal lyric, "Get Down Boogie, do you want to do it—uh?" Few people, however, went to see them for the funk stuff; Supercharge also had a comedy routine, and it was stupendous. If you've not heard "Dishes," imagine the Drifters if the *Animal House* canteen scene had got to them first. And if you have, you'll already know the bright significance of the title.

If Pub Rock was an essentially British institution, albeit one with both an American presence and some American musicians, punk was a worldwide phenomenon, with roots that likewise spanned continents (at least in rock 'n' roll terms).

It was fall 1976 before the first British bands released their debut singles, the Damned's "New Rose" (later covered by Guns N' Roses) and the Sex Pistols' "Anarchy in the UK" (ditto, Megadeth). By that time, New York's Patti Smith and the Ramones, and California's Runaways had all released albums, while Television, Wayne (later Jayne) County, Richard Hell, the Talking Heads and the Dead Boys and Pere Ubu (both from Cleveland) were preparing to follow suit.

In Australia, Radio Birdman, the Saints and the Boys Next Door, forerunners of Nick Cave's Birthday Party, were all underway; while France had already shown its strength with Little Bob Story and the Stinky Toys, the latter of whom appeared at London's legendary 100 Club Punk Festival that same September.

But the new movement blossomed quickly. Just a couple of "punk" 45s at the end of 1976 had become several hundred within a year, as the major labels hurried to scoop up the biggest bands, and a wealth of enterprising independents rose up to devour the remainder.

Punk bands were in the British chart, and selling out the biggest venues.

Across the board, it was the biggest jab in the arm that the UK music industry had experienced since the British Invasion, and maybe even bigger than that. Back then, after all, it was the major labels that called all the shots.

Now, the pioneers at Stiff and Chiswick had been joined by Beggars Banquet, Rabid, New Hormones, Small Wonder, Illegal, Step Forward, and dozens more—labels that started out, in some cases, as back- or bedroom operations, but established themselves so thoroughly that many were still active, and successful, decades later. Collecting their output, even through the early years, can be challenging, but it certainly introduces you to some fabulous music.

Neither was the excitement limited to the UK. It swiftly transpired that cities all over the United States were nurturing their own little punk

15 FABULOUS SUB POP 45s

Babes in Toyland: *House/ Arriba* (gold vinyl—Sub Pop 66, 1990): **$50**

Big Chief: *Blowout Kit/ Chrome Helmet* (white vinyl— Sub Pop SP 53, 1990): **$30**

Dinosaur Jr: *The Wagon/ Better Than Gone* (purple vinyl—Sub Pop 68, 1990): **$75**

Fugazi: *Joe #1/Break In/Song #1* (green vinyl—Sub Pop 52, 1989): **$75**

The Honeymoon Killers: *Get It Hot/Gettin' Hot* (red vinyl— Sub Pop 51, 1989): **$50**

Mudhoney: *This Gift/Baby Help Me Forget* (purple vinyl— Sub Pop 44a, 1989): **$40**

Mudhoney: *Touch Me I'm Sick/Sweet Young Thing* (Any of accidental purple, red, yellow or blueish vinyl pressings— Sub Pop 18, 1988): **$200**

Nirvana: *Love Buzz/Big Cheese* (#1 in Sub Pop Singles Club series—Sub Pop 23, 1988): **$500**

Nirvana: *Sliver/Dive* (Clear pink/ lavender vinyl—Sub Pop 73, 1990): **$60**

Screaming Trees: *Change Has Come EP* (red vinyl—Sub Pop 48, 1989): **$75**

Smashing Pumpkins: *Tristessa/La Dolly Vita* (red vinyl—Sub Pop 90, 1991): **$500**

Soundgarden: *Hunted Down/ Nothing to Say* (blue vinyl— Sub Pop 12a, 1987): **$80**

Jon Spencer Blues Explosion: *Big Yule Log Boogie/My Christmas Wish* (Mispress on clear lilac vinyl; labels claim this is "Max Gomez"—Sub Pop 180, 1992): **$60**

Tad: *Ritual Device/Daisy* (gold vinyl—Sub Pop 19, 1988): **$60**

The White Stripes: *Party of Special Things to Do/China Pig/Ashtray Heart* (Fold open sleeve; Singles Club, December 2000—Sub Pop 527, 2000): **$125**

scenes… or, at least, scenes that would be absorbed into the movement.

From Los Angeles—the Urinals, the Hollywood Squares and the Randoms; from New Orleans—the Hormones; from Cleveland—the Electric Eels and X [Blank] X; from Akron—the Bizarros and the Waitresses; from Chula Vista, California—the Zeros; from San Francisco—Tuxedo Moon and the Flaming Groovies; from Austin—the Skunks; from Philadelphia—Crash Course in Science; from Boston—Pastiche; from Seattle—the Lewd… and more.

Other bands from other cities; more bands from the same ones, Akron's Rubber City Rebels and Devo; Boston's Unnatural Axe and La Peste; and from Los Angeles again, the Germs, X, TSOL, the Weirdos, Agent Orange, the Deadbeats….

Some cut albums, some enjoyed lengthy careers. Others crashed and burned after just a single or two. The important thing is, all made their presence felt, whether across the course of a few months, or for years and decades to come.

Whereas punk in the UK was effectively over by the end of the seventies, splintering into a riot of related movements (Oi!, Anarcho-punk, and so forth), its U.S. counterpart simply honed itself in just two directions, the ferocity of hardcore (Black Flag, the Circle Jerks, the early Replacements) and an edgier, experimental fury exemplified through the 1980s by Sonic Youth and Big Black, that in turn was touted as a major influence by Nirvana, as they burst out of the Pacific Northwest as the figureheads of grunge.

By which time, of course, vinyl was all but forgotten, at least so far as albums were concerned, and *their* revolution was carried out on CD.

The decades that spread out behind them, however, are littered with vinyl treasures. Some were the work of major labels, major bands, with major backing.

Others were privately pressed in absurdly small quantities, and released on tiny independent labels that themselves might grow to become figureheads of the years to come: Twin Tone, SST, Homestead, Touch and Go, Blast First and, ultimately, Sub Pop—the label that brought us not only Nirvana, but also Mudhoney, Tad, Soundgarden, the Screaming Trees, the Afghan Whigs, the soundtrack to the early 1990s.

Any of these labels, any of these cities, any of these bands. Your collection can start wherever you like.

NIRVANA

SUNDAY OCTOBER 8 9pm
LIFTICKET 6212 Maple St.
$4

MAIN VEIN

SUB POP

CHAPTER 19

THE EIGHTIES
PICTURE DISCS AND PERFECT SOUND

THE EIGHTIES WERE THE DECADE where anything went. Fresh musical movements rose and fell on what sometimes felt like a monthly basis, as a decade that began with the last gasps of the New Wave, and its gradual shift into what was then known as College Rock (but which later became "alternative"), followed through with Two Tone ska, hip hop and rap, synthipop, gothic rock, hair metal, glam rock (and a very different beast it was to its decade-old British namesake), industrial… it felt, sometimes, as though a bunch of bands needed only change their hairstyle and put on different trousers for them to become the trailblazing prophets of a new musical religion.

Some sterling talents emerged, of course, and swiftly thrust their way toward the upper echelons of the collecting hobby. In no particular order, U2, Prince, Dead or Alive, Marc Almond, Duran Duran, the Pet Shop Boys, Metallica, Ministry, Twisted Sister, Robyn Hitchcock, REM, and many, many more, all burst through in a major way.

No longer Motown's favorite child star, Michael Jackson confirmed his place at the top of the pile with *Thriller,* one of the biggest selling records of all time. Frankie Goes to Hollywood spearheaded the ZTT label's quest for world dominance, a goal

Michael Jackson and Madonna (far right) shaped the mainstream sound and the vibe of the eighties. Herb Ritts photographed Madonna for her hit 1986 album *True Blue.*
Image courtesy Heritage Auctions

achieved by flooding the market with a still near-impenetrable jungle of twelve-inch singles, cassette-only remixes, ever-changing b-sides and a lot more besides. The twelve inch itself maintained its reign as the format of choice for so many artists.

Madonna burst onto the scene. Stevie Nicks launched her solo career, adding a fresh layer of rarities to the already jam-packed Fleetwood Mac discography. Bruce Springsteen and Queen confirmed their commercial supremacy with catalogs that routinely spun off fresh delights.

The picture disc danced into view, a 78-era technology that resurfaced briefly in the UK in the early 1970s, and then exploded outward

24 HIGH PRICED PICTURE DISCS

The Cars: *Shake It Up*
(Elektra 5E-567, 1981): **$50**

Lyda Carter: *Portrait*
(Epic 35308, 1978): **$75**

Elvis Costello: *My Aim Is True/ This Year's Model* (Columbia 0
(no cat #), 1978) current value: **$150**

Cher: *Take Me Home*
(Casablanca NBPIX-7133, 1979): **$50**

Peter Criss: *Peter Criss*
(Casablanca NBPIX-7122, 1978): **$50**

Ace Frehley: *Ace Frehley*
(Casablanca NBPIX-7121, 1978): **$50**

Judy Garland: *In Concert: San Francisco* (Mark 56 632, 1978): **$750**

Michael Jackson: *Thriller*
(Epic 8.00E+0838867, 1983): **$150**

The Jacksons: *The Jacksons*
(Epic PE34229, 1976): **$500**

Iron Maiden: *The Number of the Beast* (Capitol SEAX-12219, 1982): **$50**

Iron Maiden: *Piece of Mind*
(Capitol SEAX-12306, 1983): **$75**

Judas Priest: *Great Vinyl and Concert Hits*
(Columbia 9C939926, 1984): **$75**

Metallica: *Kill 'Em All*
(Megaforce MRI 069, 1983): **$150**

Parliament: *Motor-Booty Affair*
(Casablanca NBPIX7125, 1978): **$85**

Pink Floyd: *The Dark Side of the Moon* (Capitol SEAX-11902, 1978): **$80**

The Residents: *Freak Show*
(Ralph OP-011, 1991): **$80**

The Rolling Stones: *Through the Past, Darkly* (Big Hits Vol. 2)
(London NPS3, 1969): **$6,000**
(*only 15 copies known to exist*)

at the very end of the 1970s, as the industry seemed set upon making certain that every album of note, and a lot of singles too, became available with a photograph pressed into the vinyl itself.

Such releases were certainly marketable, especially when buyers were assured that the discs were strictly limited editions. They have long remained collectible, too, as some of those editions were genuinely small. Others, however, seemed less scarce, and suspiciously so.

As a record store buyer in London in the late 1970s, I fondly recall asking a visiting rep if I could order plain, unlimited edition, un-pictured, black vinyl pressings of a certain 45. He looked at me as though I had demanded the impossible, and so it turned out. Even after the record

Queen: ...*at the BBC*
(Hollywood ED-62005, 1995): **$150**

Queensryche: *Operation: Mindcrime* (EMI Manhattan SPRO-04136/7, 1988): **$100**

Gene Simmons: *Gene Simmons* (Casablanca NBPIX7120, 1978): **$80**

Paul Stanley: *Paul Stanley* (Casablanca NBPIX-7123, 1978): **$75**

Supertramp: *Breakfast in America* (A&M SP-3730, 1979): **$500**

Sun Ra: *Cosmo Omnibus Imaginable Illusion: Live at Pit-Inn* (DIW DIWP-2, 1988): **$300**

Stevie Ray Vaughan: *Couldn't Stand the Weather* (Epic 8.00E+0839609, 1984): **$250**

charted, and sales *surely* far exceeded the 30,000 picture discs that constituted the limited edition, not a single black disc ever crossed our threshold, and I have never seen one since then either.

Neither was I merely being deliberately contrary with my request. The fact is, as a rule, picture discs sounded horrible.

Not the first few times you played them (or not always). But give the record more than a couple of listens, and the sound would begin breaking up, growing rougher and more distorted every time the needle touched it. At which point you'd realize that picture discs were never meant to be played in the same way as an old-fashioned black vinyl record was.

They were meant to be displayed, framed on the wall and kept in pure, pristine shape for ever and ever. Or, at least, until you sold them, at which point you would discover that some picture discs are indeed much sought-after creatures. And others are scarcely worth whatever you paid for them when they were brand new.

But vinyl was not to have things all its own way. Cassette singles arose as a potential rival to the 45, while the LP found itself facing the fight of its life, as the industry unveiled the latest technology—the compact disc.

It is now over 40 years since the first compact discs appeared on the market back in 1983—as a point of interest, LPs had scarcely been around any longer by that point.

Digital technology itself was not new; Japan's NHK Technical Research Unit had a digital audio recorder up and running back in 1967; and by 1970, the Dutch company Philips had perfected a way of etching digital sound onto a glass disc, which could then be read by a laser.

The first digital audio disc prototypes debuted at the 1977 Tokyo Audio Fair, and in 1978 the specifications to which the eventual Compact Disc would adhere were laid down. And five years later, when the first discs and players were introduced in the US, some 800,000 CDs were sold during the first year alone, alongside with 30,000 CD players. In 1984, America opened its first manufacturing plant; by 1986, US sales amounted to 3 million players and 53 million discs.

The CD had arrived, and every other format was destined for oblivion.

It was not a perfect system. Visit any audiophile forum today, and you will find people arguing furiously over whether or not vinyl actually sounds better than CD, but generally agreeing that it merely sounds *different*. Which is often just as important. Because, for many listeners, all the technology in the world will never permit a digital recording or remastering to sound like a genuine analog recording, and vice versa.

That latter is the reason why so many compact discs (especially during the medium's infancy) sounded so poor; because engineers simply transferred the existing analog tapes to digital, without allowing for any of the new format's own requirements.

Neither was it the sound alone that suffered from the rise of the little silver coaster. Purchasers of early CDs of Queen's classic *Sheer Heart Attack* album were horrified to discover that the seamless suite of songs that devoured most of side one was now broken up by split-second gaps, caused by the medium's need to index each track individually.

There were other problems, too. The artwork was tiny, any liner notes minute. The first CDs had barely been sold when buyers were complaining that they could no longer read the lyric sheets. Album covers that once spread out over twelve, even twenty-four inches of tabletop were now crushed into five inch squares.

When Hawkwind released their landmark *Space Ritual* live album in 1973, the sleeve folded out into eight album-sized panels, and it looked magnificent. When the album was reissued on CD, six of those panels vanished entirely as labels cut costs by cutting all but what *they* considered the most essential parts of the packaging, the front and the back.

But still people purchased them in ever increasing numbers and, by the end of the decade, the majority of American labels had given up on vinyl production altogether. Other countries followed... it is still possible to find European vinyl releases of certain key artists pushing deep into the first half of the 1990s. But they were produced in limited quantities to begin with, and were swiftly snatched up by fans and collectors.

Only in the most recent years have we finally been able to pick up vinyl versions of some of the era's biggest hits... Nirvana's *Nevermind* and *In Utero*, Prodigy's *Fat of the Land* and the entire Oasis catalog, Britney Spears' *In The Zone*, Morrissey's *Your Arsenal*, Madonna's *Ray of Light*.

The transfer back to black has not been a flawless process. Don't get

◀ Prince's *Purple Rain* promotional cardboard stand-up, 1984.
Image courtesy Heritage Auctions

HOT SCORES

FROM THE LAST DAYS OF VINYL

Alice in Chains: *We Die Young*
(Columbia CAS2192, 1990): **$75**

Beastie Boys: *Check Your Head*
(Capitol C1-98938, 1992): **$75**

Big Black: Boxes (Touch & Go
TG111, 1992): **$150**

Cocteau Twins: *Cocteau Twins*
(Capitol SPRO79066/7, 1991): **$75**

Garth Brooks: *No Fences* (Capitol
Nashville R173266, 1990): **$75**

Guided By Voices: *Same Place
the Fly Got Smashed*
(Rocket #9 (no cat #), 1990): **$75**

Hampton Hawes: *Autumn
Leaves in Paris*
(Moon MLP-005, 1990): **$75**

Keith Jarrett: *Changeless*
(ECM 1392, 1990): **$75**

Kiss: *First Kiss, Last Licks*
(Mercury 792-1, 1990): **$150**

Madonna: *Erotica* (Maverick
PRO-A-5904, 1992): **$75**

Mazzy Star: *She Hangs
Brightly* (Rough Trade RUS771,
1990): **$150**

Metallica: *Metallica*
(Elektra 61113, 1991): **$75**

Negativland: *U2*
(SST 272, 1990): **$300**

Paul McCartney: *Tripping
the Live Fantastic*
(Capitol C1-94778, 1990): **$75**

Primus: *Frizzle Fry* (Caroline
CAROL1619, 1990): **$100**

Primus: *Suck on This*
(Caroline CAROL1620, 1990): **$75**

Selena: *16 Super Exitos
Originales* (Capitol/EMI Latin H1-
42299, 1990) current value: **$100**

Smashing Pumpkins: *Gish*
(Caroline 1705, 1991): **$75**

Soundgarden: *Badmotorfinger*
(A&M 7502153741, 1991)
current value: **$75.00**

Soundgarden: *Louder
Than Live* (A&M SP-17951,
1990): **$100**

out the lie detector, but I think the first time I ever encountered the words "digitally mastered" emblazoned across a rock LP sleeve was the German language version of Peter Gabriel's *Security* album, back in 1982, and about a year before that on some Deutsche Grammophon classicals.

It was a big deal as well. More than 30 years have passed since then, but you may still recall the excitement that was percolating through the music industry at the time, as artists and audience alike pondered the possibilities of this revolutionary new technique.

Digital sound! How could it fail to be perfect?

Today, those words are less

The Queers: *Grow Up*
(Shakin' Street 010, 1990): **$250**

U2: *Achtung Baby*
(Island 510347-1, 1991): **$150**

Uncle Tupelo: *No Depression* (Rockville 6050-1, 1990) current value: **$75**

Unsane: *...for Tennis*
(Matador OLE 009, 1991): **$150**

Wilson Phillips: *Shadows and Light* (SBK 1P-8219, 1992): **$75**

alluring. And not only because we have grown so accustomed to them that they barely elicit a shrug any longer. "Digitally mastered?" we sneer. "You and everybody else."

And "digitally *re*mastered?"

Okay, those are fighting words.

Especially when applied to vinyl.

We need not get into some great debate about the pros and cons of taking an old tape and running it through a computer program in order to improve (or otherwise) the sound quality.

Compact discs are a digital medium, and so are mp3s. If we want music we can play in those formats, then it's going to be digitized whether we like it or not.

Where things get interesting, and maybe even controversial, is when that same digital remastering is applied *back* to vinyl. When an engineer takes a recorded sound that was designed for analog, converts it to one that was designed for CD, and then converts it back to a format that was also designed for analog. It's a little like moving to France for a few years, but only learning the language after you have returned to the U.S. And then expecting everyone here to know what you are saying.

It's an old argument, of course; another of those that have been percolating in chat rooms and discussion boards ever since vinyl began making its "comeback."

With new reissues appearing every week, and some fabulous old finds being restored to the 12-inch racks, we are arguably in the same position with our musical heritage today as we were in the early 1990s, once it became apparent that CDs were not being held back only for monster big sellers, and that great swathes of even the obscurest catalog were now destined to be reissued.

Another analogy? An architect came along and completely demolished your favorite city—and twenty years on, built an identical replica on the ruins.

But flip the coin, and you will discover that many of the pathways that modern record companies take are themselves walked out of necessity.

Asked whether a new vinyl reissue should be pressed from its original analog masters, or if the manufacturer should instead employ the best-quality-possible digital remaster, some fans are adamant that only the original (or as close as possible) analog tapes should be employed.

The labels and the retailers, on the other hand, long ago noted that the more modern bells and whistles are attached to the disc, the better its chance of selling to the general public, as opposed to committed vinyl fans. The magic words "digitally remastered" do still have considerable cachet.

Some fans and collectors demand the original album be restored to as close to its primal state as possible. But others still require the bonus tracks that they grew accustomed to during the CD age.

The future worth of many of these rereleases has still to be assessed; for as

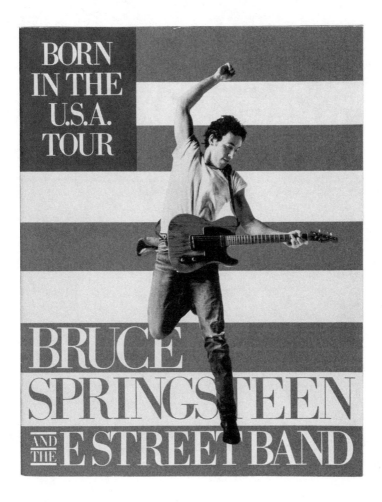

long as a record remains in print, it is worth only whatever its recommended retail price might be.

But track back to those years when vinyl was fighting a losing battle against the digital interloper, and it often shocking to see how values have soared; how records that you passed over in 1988, 1989, in favor of the CD are now selling for $50, $60 or more, while you can barely even give the corresponding CD away.

Indeed, just as long time vinyl collectors look back on the early 1990s as a golden age for bargain hunting, as the entire nation (or so it seemed) swapped out their old LPs for new CDs, so the opposite is true. CD collectors are having a whale of a time as collectors now take the same journey back again.

And probably feel rather foolish, as well. "Oh, if *only* I'd hung on to that copy of…."

CLASSICAL MUSIC IS THE DRIVING FORCE...

LUDWIG VAN BEETHOVEN

CHAPTER 20

THE CLASSICS

CLASSICAL MUSIC IS THE DRIVING force behind every significant advance in recording technology of the twentieth century… at least, those that appreciate quality over convenience.

It was the classics that spearheaded the drive to cram more and more music onto a platter, leading ultimately to the creation of the long-playing disc.

It was the classics that led the demand for stereo in the late 1950s, and quadraphonic in the early 1970s. And it was the classics that pioneered and popularized the compact disc a decade later.

And if any single group of record collectors can be said to have *truly* benefitted from the arrival of the compact disc, it was classical music enthusiasts.

Forget all the great classic *rock* albums that flooded the market as music buyers leaped aboard the new digital bandwagon; forget jazz, blues, punk and goth. Far more classical music classics hit the shelves, and vinyl fans could not believe their luck.

Classical collectors simply couldn't get enough of CDs, and with very good reason. Just as vinyl mavens have always muttered darkly about classical records looking, feeling and sounding a cut above the quality that was deemed appropriate for pop and rock fans, so CD fans feel the same way.

Something about the mastering, something about the sonics, something about… well, everything, really. Even in the earliest days of the digital

A dying Mozart sings his requiem in this illustration by Thomas W. Shields.
Image courtesy Library of Congress

medium, classical CDs routinely sounded better than rock. And they've been around longer, as well.

In August 1982—that is, *two years* before Bruce Springsteen's *Born in the USA* became the first compact disc released in America, Claude Arrau's 1979 recording of the Chopin waltzes became the first commercial CD *anywhere* (Philips 400 025-2). In fact, Arrau himself was invited to press the button that set the presses running in the first place.

Legend also insists that classical music was responsible for the very dimensions of the CD itself.

When Philips first developed the compact disc it was intended to be 11.5 cm in diameter. But Norio Ohga, Vice President of Sony, who was partnering with the Dutch company in the enterprise, demanded 12cm. And why? So a full recording of his favorite piece of music, all 74 minutes of Beethoven's *Ninth Symphony*, could be fit onto a disc. (Ironically, when Sony released its first 15 classical CDs in Japan that October, Beethoven's *Ninth* was conspicuous by its absence. His *Fifth* and *Third*, respectively, were selected instead.)

By the time Springsteen joined the party, American import stores that had chosen to import these new-fangled digital doohickeys were already overflowing with classical music... and the used stores down the road were feeling the first splashes of what would become a flood of now-unwanted classical records.

Many of which (and this is another of those imponderables upon which rock collectors will sometimes muse in the dead of night) were in infinitely better condition than you'd ever expect to find an obviously much-loved and well-played record to be in.

Yes, it needs to be said. In general, classical collectors seem to *care* for their records a lot better than the rest of us.

You can find proof of that any place used records are for sale. Plow through the rock, pop, jazz, folk, reggae and R&B sections, and you will encounter any manner of flaws and failings. But move to the classical racks, and disc after disc will appear VG+ at the least.

Older box sets may show some shelf wear; those that originally retailed at budget prices, or held more discs than the cardboard could reasonably sustain, will certainly have split seams and torn edges. But that's a consequence of the manufacturing process, not the box's treatment thereafter. The discs inside will invariably look, and sound, great.

One could if so disposed, hypothesize on why this should be.

Are classical lovers less likely to throw parties, at which their records are strewn across the floor, to be stepped on by clumsy dancers? (Answer: probably).

Are they more prone to listen to a piece of music all the way through, rather than constantly raising and lowering the needle to find their favorite tracks? (Answer: again, probably.)

One could then wander through a variety of contentious, but nevertheless convincing demographic factors (age, income, etc.), and even consider a canard that appears so often on sundry Internet forums that there must be a degree of truth to it—the belief that "serious" classical collectors will rarely purchase a used record or CD, unless there is simply no way a particular recording can be located in a particular format.

Late in the 1980s, for example, Deutsche Grammophon released a series of digitally recorded Mahler symphonies on both CD and vinyl, but with the latter in such limited quantities that, if you didn't buy them within a few days of release, you were unlikely ever to find them again. As shown by the following list of the label's most expensive collectibles, that early failure will cost a lot to remedy today.

TOP 10
DEUTSCHE GRAMMOPHON
RARITIES

Johanna Martzy, Jean Antonietti, Dika Newlin, Yaltah Menuhin and Michael Mann: *Maurice Ravel & c.* (Mono, LPEM 19126, 1958): **$800**

Leonard Bernstein: *Mahler Symphony No.6* (2LP, 427 697-1, 1989): **$700**

Martzy: *Works By Ravel Milhaud Falla* (DGM 19126, 1958): **$500**

Deutsche Grammophon Avant Garde Vol.4 (6LP box set, 2720 038, 1971): **$400**

Henryk Szeryng: *Johann Sebastian Bach—6 Sonaten Und Partiten Für Violine Solo* (3LP, 2709 028, 1970): **$350**

Leonard Bernstein: *Mahler Symphony No.2* (2LP, 423-396 423-497, 1988): **$350**

Anja Thauer: *Dvorak—Konzert für Violoncello* (139392, 1968): **$300**

Mainardi, Borciani: *Schubert Sonata D.821* (10-inch, DG 17157, 1952): **$300**

Deutsche Grammophon Avant Garde Vol.1 (6LP box set, 104 988/93, 1968): **$300**

Beethoven Edition 1970 (12 Box Sets, 1-12, 1970): **$300**

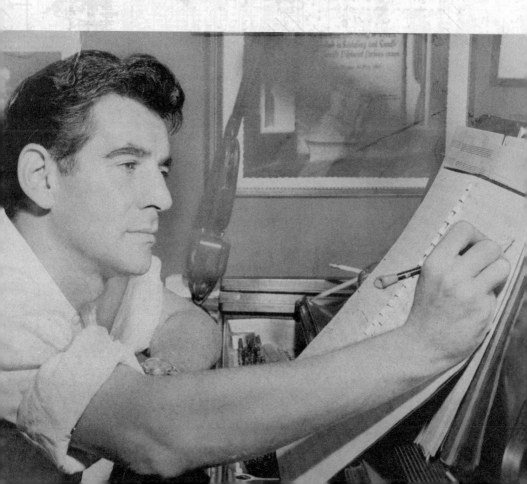

So yes, when classical records appear on the used market, they tend to have had just one previous, careful, owner, and they are in more or less pristine condition.

None of which means you *won't* find classics that have been scratched into a state of unlistenable white noise. Just that it's not at all difficult to find one that hasn't.

Another factor that comes into play is that classical records are less... what is the word? It's certainly inaccurate to say they are less collectible or collected; likewise, they are probably better-studied than any other field in recorded music (jazz notwithstanding).

But they are less *understood* by the general market. Take 20 rock rarities into your local used store and watch the dealer's eyes light up. Take twenty classical rarities to the same store and you might not even make a sale.

The majority of general record dealers just glaze over when they are offered a classical collection. Maybe they'll give a second glance to certain labels (everyone's heard of Deutche Grammophon, for example), but all that means is they'll put a $5 sticker on the sleeve, as opposed to the $2 that everything else will receive.

Part of the reason for this is simple. There's just *so much* of it! How many times has Beethoven's *5th Symphony* have been released over the past century? Hundreds, certainly. Thousands, maybe. Tens of thousands, conceivably, and all spread across more record labels than you've ever heard of, from the scrappiest no-name budget concern, to the most glorious audiophiliac outfit.

How can anybody pull them apart?

The answer is the one you were probably expecting: Experience. Knowledge. No less than in any other field, longtime collectors know instinctively how to separate the wheat from the chaff, in terms of performance, performer, label, liner notes, the lot. In exactly the same way, in fact, as a Beatles collector knows that an early pressing Capitol LP is always going to be worth more than, say, the umpteenth go-round for the Star Club live tapes, pumped out by another budget label.

But there are still dealers out there who don't know the difference, and wonder why nobody wants to purchase their wares....

Anybody looking to start a classical collection from scratch, of course, is best advised to haunt those places where the albums line up unwanted and seemingly, unsale-able, for a buck or two a pop. Grab the names you recognize, and take a chance on those that you don't.

It's a vast field, after all. Indeed, if you subscribe to the belief that rock 'n' roll is far too vague a term to encompass all that has been

◀ Leonard Bernstein making annotations to a musical score in 1954.
Image courtesy Library of Congress

accomplished in popular music over the past sixty years, imagine how the classical connoisseur feels, seeing six centuries or more lumped together beneath that one catch-all.

For it is true. Dig through any random selection of used "classical" records, and you are as likely to discover the earliest volumes in the DG subsidiary Archiv Produktion's *History of Music* series, tapping thirteenth century chant and song, as you are the decidedly twentieth century offerings of Philip Glass and Gavin Bryars.

True, the music therein was not recorded that long ago. But it was written and first performed back then, and the "modern" recordings are as faithful to those prototypes as it is possible to be. Look out for the works of David Munrow and his Early Music Consort of London, released in the U.S. by such labels as Musical Heritage Society, London and Angel; or, again, the aforementioned Archiv Produktion's series.

As for the earliest *recordings*, the first thing to remember is that neither the medium nor the available recording methods were especially conducive to classical music until the mid 1920s. Two-sided discs did not really come into use until 1908 (although occasional issues had been appearing since 1904); furthermore, until 1925 and the advent of electronic recording, records were cut live, with the artist literally standing or sitting by the recording horn, watching the record cut as he or she performed.

Vocal selections from the classics, of course, proliferated, and in 1917, the Philadelphia Symphony Orchestra debuted on Victor Red Seal with recordings of Brahms' Hungarian Dances numbers five and six, and Anitra's Dance from *Peer Gynt*.

Brahms

The following year, the Boston Symphony Orchestra was recorded across a handful of releases by the same label—the Prelude to Act 3 of Wagner's *Lohengrin*, the Marche Miniature from the *Nutcracker Suite*, and the Finale from the *1812 Overture* (necessarily spread across both sides of the record). The New York Philharmonic commenced its recording career in 1923; the San Francisco Symphony Orchestra in 1925.

But not until the advent of the long-playing record at the end of the 1940s did the classics truly explode onto the market, with the first microgroove LP pressing released being the Mendelssohn *Violin Concerto in E Minor* with soloist Nathan Milstein, and Bruno Walter conducting the

Philharmonic Symphony Orchestra of New York (Columbia ML4001). For historical reasons alone, copies of this are routinely valued at $150 today.

The series then continued as follows:

Bach: *Violin Concertos—Busch Chamber Players* (Columbia ML 4002): **$85**

Beethoven: *Piano Sonatas 8 and 14—Rudolf Serkin* (Columbia ML 4003): **$100**

Beethoven: *Piano Concerto No. 5—Serkin / Walter / NY Philharmonic* (Columbia ML 4004): **$100**

Beethoven: *Quartet No 1 in F Maj. Op. 18—Budapest String Quartet* (Columbia ML 4005): **$80**

Beethoven: *Quartet No 15 in A min. Op. 132—Budapest String Quartet* (Columbia ML 4006): **$100**

Beethoven: *Sonata No. 9 for Piano and Violin Op. 47 Kreutzer- Busch / Serkin* (Columbia ML 4007): **$50**

Beethoven: *Symphony No. 4—Szell / Cleveland Orchestra* (Columbia ML 4008): **$80**

Beethoven: *Symphony No. 5—Walter / NY Philharmonic* (Columbia ML 4009): **$80**

Beethoven: *Symphony No. 6—Walter / Philadelphia Orchestra* (Columbia ML 4010): **$70**

Beethoven: *Symphony No. 7—Ormandy / Philadelphia Orchestra* (Columbia ML 4011): **$50**

Beethoven: *Violin Concerto In D Major—Szigeti / Walter* (Columbia ML 4012): **$50**

Bizet: *Carmen Excerpts* (Columbia ML 4013): **$60**

Brahms: *Piano Concerto No. 2 in B flat—Serkin / Ormandy / Philadelphia Orchestra* (Columbia ML 4014): **$60**

Brahms: *Violin Concerto in D—Szigeti / Ormandy / Philadelphia Orchestra* (Columbia ML 4015): **$80**

Brahms: *Symphony No. 1—Rodzinski / NY Philharmonic* (Columbia ML 4016): **$100**

Brahms: *Symphony No. 4 In E Minor, Op. 98—Ormandy / Philadelphia Orchestra* (Columbia ML 4017): **$100**

Debussy: *Quartet In G Minor, Op. 10—Budapest String Quartet* (Columbia ML 4018): **$80**

Debussy: *Preludes—Robert Casadesus* (Columbia ML 4019): **$70**

Debussy: *Two Nocturnes / Respighi: Pines of Rome—Ormandy / Philadelphia Orchestra* (Columbia ML 4020): **$80**

GERSHWIN

DEBUSSY

Debussy: *Iberia / Ravel: La Valse—Reiner / Pittsburgh Symphony Orchestra* (Columbia ML 4021): **$100**

Dvorak: *Concerto in B Minor for Cello—Piatigorsky—Ormandy / Philadelphia Orchestra* (Columbia ML 4022): **$50**

Dvorak: *Symphony No. 5 'New World'—Ormandy / Philadelphia Orchestra* (Columbia ML 4023): **$50**

Franck: *Symphony In D Minor—Ormandy / Philadelphia Orchestra* (Columbia ML 4024): **$80**

Gershwin: *Concerto in F for Piano and Orchestra—Levant—Kostelanetz / NY Philharmonic* (Columbia ML 4025): **$60**

Of course Columbia did not have the field to itself for long, with a host of rival labels swiftly arising to challenge their dominance of both the long-playing scene in general, and the classical genre in particular.

Of them all, it was Deutsche Grammophon who positioned themselves at the very forefront of the genre, a German company founded in 1898 by Emile and Joseph Berliner, the pioneers of the flat disc that upended Edison's cylinder recordings.

A European force throughout the 78 era, DG remained at the forefront of recording technology throughout that span, perfecting (among other things) the variable grooves technique that allowed a single 78 to host up to nine minutes of music. That was in 1950; the following year, the company produced its first LP, Mendelssohn's *Midsummer Night's Dream*, performed by the Berlin Philharmonic beneath the baton of Eugen Jochum.

For many people, collectors and otherwise, DG is the most familiar classical label in the world, and the most collected as well, a status which is well-deserved.

In terms of performance, the best of the label's output can be compared favorably with that of any of its rivals. True, many collectors feel that the actual sound quality pales in comparison with various rival concerns (RCA Red Seal, London/Decca, the UK's EMI family), but in terms of performance, DG cannot be beat.

Again, there are dozens, if not hundreds, of alternate versions of almost every release in the DG catalog, but there is something almost reassuring, a trademark of quality if you will, about that familiar yellow logo— particularly throughout the period where it spread across the top third-or-so of the front cover and spine. The sheer uniformity of a carefully curated DG collection is itself a beauty to behold.

Other labels have their adherents, however—of course they do. The British Decca label made an early and very pronounced impact on the classical vinyl scene and, like DG, has celebrated that with a splendid CD box set rounding up the best of their 1950s mono output.

Furthermore, Decca's U.S equivalent, London, shares the same high qualities as the UK releases. In fact, unusually, London's releases utilized the exact same masters as their British counterparts.

Pursuing these early recordings (both those included in the box sets and those that missed the cut) in their original vinyl incarnations is not an easy project, but it is certainly a rewarding one.

The Angel label, established in New York by EMI in 1953, was responsible for issuing some 500 highly rated British classical (and occasionally other) recordings over the next few years; while you will often find RCA Red Seal being praised for producing the best sounding albums of all, and a listen through the catalog will leave you in full agreement.

There again, how can you fail to leave an eternal impact when you're releasing recordings by three of the most acclaimed conductors of the first half of the last century (and beyond)? Serge Koussevitzky, Leopold Stokowski and Arturo Toscanini all called Red Seal home.

The famed folk label Vanguard initially focused on classical following its foundation in 1950, and over 100 releases on its Bach Guild subsidiary are rated among the finest performances of that composer's canon.

And so on.

But labels are only one way to go. Again addressing beginners, one can concentrate on individual composers (much of this book was written to the accompaniment of Dvorak, Grieg and Rangstrom); on favorite conductors, soloists or orchestras; on specific time frames.

One recent correspondent even acknowledged pursuing classical pieces that initially caught his attention via various rock bands' recreations, a fascination that developed from a 1972 RCA pressing of Mussourgsky's *Pictures at an Exhibition*, whose cover art (and liner notes) proclaimed it the music that inspired Emerson Lake & Palmer's 1971 live LP.

And one can visit the Internet in search of those sites that claim to list the "top ten" (or whatever) classical albums that "everybody should own." But remember, there are almost as many of these lists out there as there are albums in the first place, and many of them are strangely biased toward

TOP 10 CLASSICAL RARITIES

Leonid Kogans and Elisabeth Gillels: *Sonatas for Two Violins* (Columbia SAX 2531, 1964): **$6,000**

Mozart a Paris (7LP box set, Pathé DTX 191/7, 1955): **$4,000**

Michael Rabin: *The Magic Bow* (Capitol Records test pressing, 1959): **$2,500**

Jacques Dumont: *Bach—Les oeuvres pour violon Volume I, II, and III* (Belvedere BWV 1001-1006, 196?): **$2,500**

Michael Rabin: *Mosaics* (Capitol SP-8506, 1959): **$2,000**

André Cluytens: *Ravel Complete Orchestral Works* (4LP box set Columbia SAX 2476-9, 1963): **$1,500**

Noel Lee & Paul Makanowitzky: *Bach: Intégrale des sonates pour piano et violon* (Lumen unknown cat, 1959): **$1,500**

David Oistrakh: *Encores* (Columbia SAX 2253, 1954): **$1,200**

Ruggiero Ricci: *Carmen Fantaisie etc* (Decca SXL 2197 ED1, 1960): **$1,000**

Ida Haendel with Gerald Moore: *A Recital of Works...* (HMV CLP 1021, 195?): **$1,000**

recordings from the fifties and sixties, all but ignoring the fact that some remarkable recordings have been made in the decades since then.

Claudio Abbado's 1977 *Carmen*, with the young Plácido Domingo as Don José; Carlos Kleiber and the Wiener Philharmoniker's 1980 rendering of Brahms' *Symphony No.4*; Herbert Von Karajan and, again, the Wiener Philharmoniker performing Bruckner's *Symphony No.8* (1988)… ah, but here we go ourselves, making lists of "recommended" recordings, and taking all of the fun out of blindly purchasing a hatchback full of dollar bin delights and embarking upon your own voyage of discovery.

And, who knows? Somewhere within that pile of unappreciated wax, there might well lurk a *real* find!

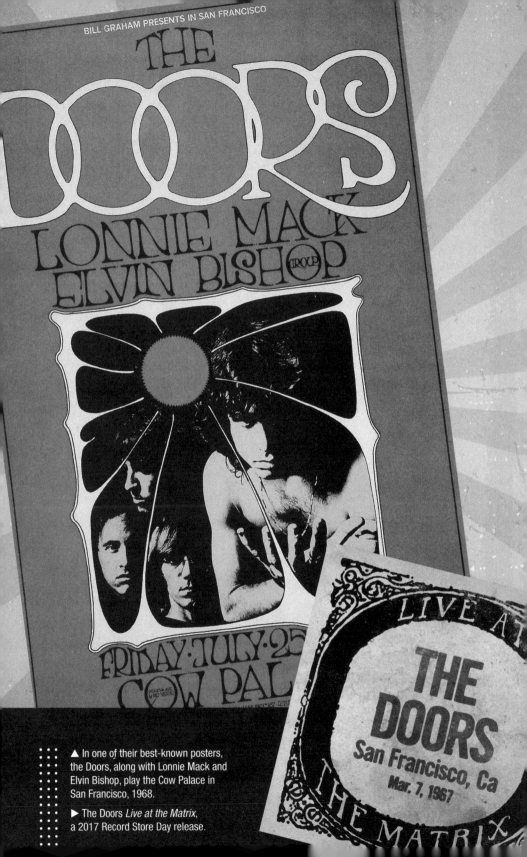

BILL GRAHAM PRESENTS IN SAN FRANCISCO

THE DOORS
LONNIE MACK
ELVIN BISHOP GROUP

FRIDAY · JULY · 25
COW PAL

LIVE AT
THE DOORS
San Francisco, Ca
Mar. 7, 1967

THE MATRIX

▲ In one of their best-known posters, the Doors, along with Lonnie Mack and Elvin Bishop, play the Cow Palace in San Francisco, 1968.

▶ The Doors *Live at the Matrix*, a 2017 Record Store Day release.

CHAPTER 21

RECORD COLLECTING TODAY

THERE WAS A TIME WHEN an artist's discography was, more or less, the body of work they created for release throughout their recorded lifetime.

Not any longer.

The Quicksilver Messenger Service released seven studio albums and two live recordings between 1968 and 1975, when they broke up. Today, there's at least 14 further live albums to add to the pile.

Jefferson Airplane put out seven studio albums, two live sets and a compilation before they turned into Jefferson Starship. Today, there's in the region of a dozen further live shows available, and a veritable groaning shelf full of compilations.

The Doors were responsible for eight albums (including the in-concert *Absolutely Live* and the compilation *13*) during Jim Morrison's lifetime; his bandmates released two more following his death. Today, there are at least

FRUITS DE MER RECORDS

THE MOST COLLECTIBLE LABEL OF THE 21ST CENTURY?

Various Artists: *A Phase We're Going Through* (pink marble vinyl): **$500**

The Chemistry Set: *The Endless More And More* (LP/CD box set with test tube, stamps, etc): **$450**

Various Artists: *Friends Of The Fish* (lathe-cut 7-inch single): **$400**

Vibravoid: *What Colour Is* (7-inch EP, purple vinyl): **$350**

Vibravoid: *Krautrock Sensation EP* (purple vinyl): **$350**

Sendelica: *Live at Crabstock* (box set, orange vinyl): **$300**

Various Artists: *Postcards From The Deep* (7-inch box set+USB): **$300**

The Pretty Things: *Live at the 100 Club* (test pressing): **$250**

Us and Them: *Julia Dreams of All The Pretty Little Horses EP* (charcoal vinyl): **$200**

Stay: *Rainy Day Mushroom Pillow EP* (gold vinyl): **$200**

40 albums, largely made up of compilations and further live recordings.

The Grateful Dead released 22 core catalog albums between 1966 and 1990… to which can be added some 130 archive live performances issued in the years since then.

Frank Zappa issued 62 albums throughout his lifetime. Almost 50 more have appeared since his death.

Now multiply even those basic numbers by every band that has ever enjoyed a significant career, and whose audience apparently never stops demanding more music, and one thing quickly becomes obvious. You will probably *never* complete your collection.

As we saw in the chapter about box sets, the vast majority of these archival offerings were initially released on compact disc; most, in fact, can still be found only in that format, as is the case for similar sets coming out today. And for very good reason, as guitarist Steve Hillage reminds us.

Hillage saw his entire catalog released in a 22-disc box set in late 2016, a set that supplemented his regular releases with mass of unreleased studio and live material.

Remembering that it can take up to four sides of vinyl to duplicate all the music that can be squeezed onto a CD, Hillage laughs, "you wouldn't be able to pick the vinyl box up! And can you imagine what the shipping costs would be?"

Large vinyl box sets have appeared, of course, and no doubt they will continue to do so. For the most part, however, vinyl remains best suited to exactly the same releases as it always has been—new releases by current artists, rereleases for past favorites, and only the occasional dip into the deeper archives.

But many of Quicksilver's posthumous live albums, and a number of the

Fish Rising, the 1975 solo debut album of English guitarist Steve Hillage.

Grateful Dead's have now been reissued as double album vinyl packages, while Jimi Hendrix's vinyl catalog, too, is slowly but surely swelling.

Which is great because, not only are we getting the music on vinyl, we're also getting album art that we can truly appreciate once again. Across the board, the resurgence of vinyl has seen a return to the artistic glories of the past. In fact, the quest for authenticity is so great that some record sleeves (the 2016 Pink Floyd reissues among them) even reproduce the folded tabs that once glued a record's front cover to the back! True, they are printed, as opposed to genuinely gummed, but the thought was there.

The picture disc has returned, and this time it arrived with none of the sonic baggage that haunted its forebears. Advances in record production appear to have rendered picture discs just as reliable as traditional black discs, and the same is said for colored vinyl too.

That, too, was often seen as problematic during the format's late 1970s/early 1980s flowering, with certain colors (yellow, orange and brown) generally regarded as the worst conveyors of pristine sound. Whether or not that was genuinely true is difficult to say. Today, however, some startlingly good-sounding records are being produced on some remarkably bizarre color combinations.

Again, it comes down to the amount of care and attention that many labels put into their releases, particularly smaller "boutique" style companies like Tompkins Square, Cuneiform and Sundazed in the US, or Britain's Fruits de Mer Records and Mega Dodo.

Stunning artwork, weighty wax, quality cardboard. Gone are the days when LPs were mass produced slices of wafer slotted into cheapo cardboard sleeves. For the first time since, perhaps, the psychedelic and progressive booms of the late 1960s/early 1970s, an album's presentation is paramount and, with it, a perceived sense of value. The impression that you're buying something that all concerned actually labored over, and taken painstaking care to create.

Maybe we *needed* vinyl to slip away for a couple of decades to remind us precisely what we were losing. CDs and mp3s are a lot more convenient, of course. They require a fraction of the storage space, and they weigh a lot less, as well. Plus, the bad old days of having to leave your seat every 15 to 20 minutes to flip over a disc are all but forgotten.

But at what cost? It's only when you become reacquainted with an old friend on vinyl that you realize how inadequate it both sounded and looked on CD all these years. If you want to *live* your music, and feel it living with you, vinyl is the only way to go.

The rise of vinyl has achieved something else, too. It has sent the hobby of record collecting through the roof, and new discoveries are as much a part of that boom as any "classic rock" reissue program you can name.

An example. Sleaze formed back in 1975, five teenagers from England's most southwestern extremity linking in a band whose influences ranged from the glam of Cockney Rebel and the Doctors of Madness, to the prog of Genesis and Peter Hammill, and onto the psychedelia of Hendrix.

Slam that little combination together and a truly remarkable sound emerged, one which toured around the band's immediate locale for a year or so, then bade farewell via a trip to a nearby studio to record five of the band's best songs. Only five, because Sleaze did not go in for short, sharp pop songs. Every track was an epic, every track extended all the players to the limits of their considerable abilities.

Fifty copies were pressed for distribution to the band's fans and friends, and it is from one of that 50... whose numbers have certainly since been depreciated by time and accident... that New York's Sing Sing label repressed *Sleaze* back in 2012.

A few changes were wrought. The original release came in a plain white sleeve with a plain white label. The reissue retrieves some photos of the band (which are almost as scarce as the original vinyl) and adds liner notes by singer TV Smith. Yes, the same TV Smith who, two years later, was leading the Adverts to punk rock shaped glory (and revising one of Sleaze's songs, "Listen Don't Think," as the somewhat less extravagant "New Boys"); the same TV Smith who is now regarded among that scene's most vibrant songwriters, and workaholic live performers.

And it sounds glorious. "It was a transfer from the original vinyl," Smith explains, "and then some re-mastering.... Well, mastering actually, as I don't think the original actually got mastered."

You are highly unlikely ever to find an original copy of *Sleaze*; and you will never find it on CD, cassette or legal download. It is available *only* on vinyl, and though the market for the album is probably still minute, multiply whatever that audience might be by the number of other, similar, releases that recent years have hauled from darkest obscurity and you're suddenly looking at a very vibrant underground.

The most significant manifestation of this statement, of course, is Record Store Day (RSD). Now a twice-yearly event, RSD launched in 2008 to celebrate the array of "mom-and-pop" record stores around the country by encouraging labels and artists to create limited edition releases that would be available only on the day.

The majority of earliest participants were independent labels and, despite complaints that RSD has since expanded into a major label feeding frenzy, "indies" continue to be responsible for the majority of RSD releases. Furthermore, the after-market (online auction sites in particular) illustrate the wild popularity of the event, with many releases selling for far above their retail price within *hours* of going on sale.

Many of them, after all, are genuinely limited editions, and with every conceivable vinyl gimmick and permutation being rolled out for the event, it can often be hard to resist a particularly striking item whatever the price.

But there are many more that can now be found for considerably less than their original retail price, which reminds us of what seems to have been a continuing theme throughout this book—just because a record is rare or hard to find, that doesn't mean it's necessarily expensive.

Some, however, are.

And, at the end of the day, that is what it comes down to.

Look for what you're looking for, and buy what you think is fairly priced.

A collection does not need to be completed in a day, or even a year. (Almost) everything you want is out there somewhere, it's just a matter of waiting for it, and if a record you need feels overpriced, or over-graded, the chances are that it probably is.

This is *your* collection, after all. And only *you* know what belongs in it.

20 RECORD STORE DAY RARITIES

U2: *Songs of Innocence*
(RSD 2015, 5,000 limited edition): **$1,000**

Paul McCartney: *Sweet Thrash*
(RSD 2015, promo white label): **$1,000**

Type O Negative: *None More Negative* (RSD 2011, 1,000 limited edition green vinyl box set): **$900**

The Cure: *Friday I'm In Love*
(RSD 2012, 100 limited edition): **$800**

Cake: *Vinyl Box Set* (RSD 2014): **$750**

Dave Matthews Band: *Live Trax*
(RSD 2014): **$700**

Jack White: *Sixteen Saltines*
(a 12-inch liquid-filled record; RSD 2012): **$700**

Brand New: *Deja Entendu*
(RSD 2015): **$600**

Haim: *Better Off* (RSD 2013, 100 copies limited edition): **$500**

Metallica: *Beyond Magnetic*
(Vinyl Test Pressing; RSD 2014): **$500**

Elvis Presley: *Showroom Internationale* (RSD 2014): **$500**

De La Soul & J Dilla: *Smell The Da.I.S.Y.* (12", RSD 2014): **$500**

Mudhoney: *On Top* (test pressing, RSD 2014): **$500**

Ed Banger: *The Bee Sides*
(5 x 7" box, RSD 2011): **$500**

Elton John: *Bennie & the Jets*
(RSD 2013, 100 copies limited edition 7-inch) **$500**

Pink Floyd: *1965—Their First Recordings* (RSD 2016, 1,050 copies limited edition): **$500**

Paul McCartney: *Nineteen Hundred And Eighty Five*
(RSD 2016): **$400**

Red House Painters: *4AD numbered LP Box Set* (RSD 2015): **$400**

Heartworn Highways: *40th Anniversary Edition Wood Box Set* (RSD 2016, 1,500 copies limited edition): **$400**

David Bowie: *Starman*
(7-inch picture disc, RSD 2012) **$350**

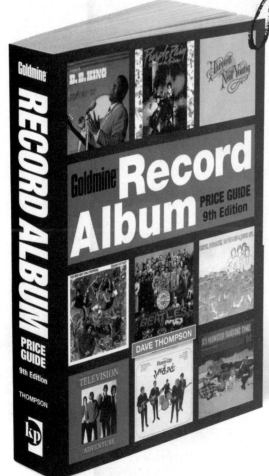